PRAISE F

Twelve Steps with Jesus

In *Twelve Steps with Jesus,* Don Williams shares the tenderness of Christ's heart toward each of us, His brokenhearted people. This breakthrough book brings to light the simple truth that we are all addicted, and Jesus came to set us free. I encourage you to begin or continue your process of healing and let Christ's amazing love wash over you with *Twelve Steps with Jesus.*

Bob Hasson
PRESIDENT AND CEO, RM HASSON, INC.

In this enjoyable, upbeat and powerful book, Don Williams uses personal experience, lively prose and understandable theory to captivate us with the revelation that nearly everyone is addicted. Lovingly, and with clarity, he points to the power, grace and love of God that is found in a personal relationship with Jesus. Using real life examples, Don gives practical and workable ways to access divine help and he reinvigorates the time-honored 12 steps. This work is so good and full of hope for those of us who are trying to cope with the modern epidemic of drug misuse. A must-read book for all who recognize the destructive power of addiction in their lives or those they seek to help.

Peter Hill, M.D.
GENERAL PRACTITIONER

Don Williams thoroughly integrates a contemporary, therapeutic understanding of recovery with a deeply insightful theology of the freedom that salvation in Christ provides. If you could read only one book to give you the practical tools of experiencing true liberation, this thoughtful, biblical book is the one you should read.

Rich Nathan
SENIOR PASTOR, VINEYARD CHURCH
COLUMBUS, OHIO

In *Twelve Steps with Jesus,* Don Williams offers a clear path of hope and healing for a new generation enslaved to addiction. This book is relevant to anyone ready to discover the freedom they were intended for. In his honest and conversational style, Don navigates the spiritual, emotional and physical dimensions of addiction in ways that clarify the big picture of this common battleground. Along the way, he not only exposes our bondage to modern idols but also leads us to practical and powerful steps toward life beyond chains.

Todd Proctor
LEAD PASTOR, ROCK HARBOR CHURCH
COSTA MESA, CALIFORNIA

Once I started reading, I couldn't put this book down—*Twelve Steps with Jesus* flows easily with gripping illustrations. Here is the A-word gently uncovered. This is a book about addictions of every kind; but it is also a book of hope. Don Williams points the way to freedom. Every home should have a copy of this book.

Bishop David Pytches

Whether it is drugs, sex, possessions or the latest business deal, we are all addicted to the cravings of sinful man. Worst of all, we probably don't know it! Don Williams paints a compelling picture of how we find our self-worth and justify our lives through false idols. Yet, if we are willing to do our inner homework, we can allow Jesus into our personal story and let the healing power of the Holy Spirit write a new chapter in our hearts. Don writes a passionate and practical book that lays out the steps to wholeness and freedom in Christ. As someone who is addicted to success, I love *Twelve Steps with Jesus!*

Vince Sicillano
PRESIDENT AND CEO, FIRST PACIFIC BANK

In *Twelve Steps with Jesus*, Don Williams confronts the fear and despair that give birth to our addictions with a message of hope, freedom and joy. The answers he gives are not found in faddish psychobabble. Rather, he says, the solutions to our addictions are found in the ancient story of redemption as given in Holy Scripture. With characteristic simplicity and clarity, Don leads us into a Christ-centered 12-step program. I heartily recommend *Twelve Steps with Jesus* to all who are searching for freedom from the tyranny of addiction.

Berten A. Waggoner
NATIONAL DIRECTOR, THE VINEYARD CHURCHES

I have great admiration for Don as a teacher and leader, as well as a friend. In *Twelve Steps with Jesus*, Don gives practical, helpful and insightful tools to remind us of our desperate need for the Cross. This book encouraged and stirred me once again to my need for the freedom that Christ desires to give us all.

Christy Wimber
VINEYARD CHRISTIAN FELLOWSHIP
ANAHEIM, CALIFORNIA

12 STEPS WITH JESUS

DON WILLIAMS

Regal

From Gospel Light
Ventura, California, U.S.A.

PUBLISHED BY REGAL BOOKS
FROM GOSPEL LIGHT
VENTURA, CALIFORNIA, U.S.A.
PRINTED IN THE U.S.A.

Regal Books is a ministry of Gospel Light, a Christian publisher dedicated to serving the local church. We believe God's vision for Gospel Light is to provide church leaders with biblical, user-friendly materials that will help them evangelize, disciple and minister to children, youth and families.

It is our prayer that this Regal book will help you discover biblical truth for your own life and help you meet the needs of others. May God richly bless you.

For a free catalog of resources from Regal Books/Gospel Light, please call your Christian supplier or contact us at 1-800-4-GOSPEL *or* www.regalbooks.com.

All Scripture quotations, unless otherwise indicated, are taken from the *Holy Bible, New International Version®.* Copyright © 1973, 1978, 1984 by International Bible Society. Used by permission of Zondervan Publishing House. All rights reserved.

Other versions used are
KJV—King James Version. Authorized King James Version.
NASB—Scripture taken from the NEW AMERICAN STANDARD BIBLE,, Copyright © 1960, 1962, 1963, 1968, 1971, 1972, 1973, 1975, 1977, 1995 by The Lockman Foundation. Used by permission.
NKJV—Scripture taken from the *New King James Version.* Copyright © 1979, 1980, 1982 by Thomas Nelson, Inc. Used by permission. All rights reserved.
RSV—From the *Revised Standard Version* of the Bible, copyright 1946, 1952, and 1971 by the Division of Christian Education of the National Council of the Churches of Christ in the U.S.A. Used by permission.
TLB—Scripture quotations marked (*TLB*) are taken from *The Living Bible,* copyright © 1971. Used by permission of Tyndale House Publishers, Inc., Wheaton, IL 60189. All rights reserved.

Any omission of credits is unintentional. The publisher requests documentation for future printings.

Cover design by Terry Dugan Design
Edited by Amy Spence

Library of Congress Cataloging-in-Publication Data
Williams, Don, 1937–
   Twelve steps with Jesus / Don Williams.
      p. cm.
   Includes bibliographical references (p.   ).
   ISBN 0-8307-3498-8
   1. Twelve-step programs—Religious aspects—Christianity. 2. Addicts—Religious life. I. Title.
BV4596.T88W55 2004
248.8'629—dc22   2004006218

   3   4   5   6   7   8   9   10   /   10   09   08   07

Rights for publishing this book in other languages are contracted by Gospel Light Worldwide, the international nonprofit ministry of Gospel Light. Gospel Light Worldwide also provides publishing and technical assistance to international publishers dedicated to producing Sunday School and Vacation Bible School curricula and books in the languages of the world. For additional information, visit www.gospellightworldwide.org; write to Gospel Light Worldwide, P.O. Box 3875, Ventura, CA 93006; or send an e-mail to info@gospellightworldwide.org.

The Twelve Steps are reprinted and adapted with permission of Alcoholics Anonymous World Services, Inc. (A.A.W.S.) The adaptation has been inserted by the inclusion of additional bracket language. Permission to reprint and adapt the Twelve Steps does not mean that A.A.W.S. has reviewed or approved the contents of this publication, or that A.A.W.S. necessarily agrees with the views expressed herein. A.A. is a program of recovery from alcoholism only—use of the Twelve Steps in connection with programs and activities which are patterned after A.A., but which address other problems, or in any other non-A.A. context, does not imply otherwise. Additionally, while A.A. is a spiritual program, A.A. is not affiliated or allied with any sect, denomination, or specific religious belief.

Contents

STEP 1

Discover Your Story

Is this book for you? Psychiatrist Gerald May says, "We are all addicts in every sense of the word."[1] But you may reply, "Not me, Don." Remember, denial is the first symptom of addiction. If we are all addicts—not only those who are alcoholics, druggies, and bingers—what do we mean by "addiction"?

We have all experienced a desire for substances (like coffee, sugar, alcohol, street drugs, prescription medications, food) or processes (like exercise, gambling, sex, work) or relationships (like parents, children, spouses, friends), and we feel we can't live without them. We use them to alter our moods, lift our depression and free us to be more ourselves. We medicate the emptiness, loneliness and pain in our lives through them. We use them to find our self-worth, justify our lives and validate what we do and even who we are. They become functional idols—the real objects of our worship. We end up powerless over them.

Unlike the ancients, we don't run off to the temples of Aphrodite or Apollo for sexual arousal, we simply hit the magazine stands, watch late-night cable TV or surf the Internet. We thumb through women's magazines for tips on how to accomplish the next seduction or keep our partner happy and excited in bed. Ah, you say, good Christians don't do this. Are you sure? Jimmy Bakker, former TV evangelist, reports that 80 percent of all the men he talks to in Pentecostal churches struggle with pornography. If sex isn't your issue, what about overeating? Why is it that so many churchgoers are clearly overweight? Why is it that as they use food, food "uses" them, and they are either on a constant cycle of bingeing and dieting or have just given up? And what about our obsessions with people? Churches are filled with gossip, dysfunctional relationships, power struggles, cliques, pecking orders—and this brokenness is fed by our addictions to each other. May writes, "To be human is to be addicted and to be addicted is to be in need of grace."[2]

Once we get out of denial, we realize that our addictions have power over us. We are in bondage, and sheer moral will cannot set us free. But is this biblical? You bet. Paul wrote:

> I don't understand myself at all, for I really want to do what is right, but I can't. I do what I don't want to— what I hate. I know perfectly well that what I am doing is wrong, and my bad conscience proves that I agree with these laws I am breaking. But I can't help myself. . . . No matter which way I turn I can't make myself do right. I want to but I can't (Rom. 7:15-18, *TLB*).

Sound familiar? It does if you have ever said, "I'll never lie again." "This is my last drink." "I'll never have another cigarette." "I am going to get my weight down and keep it down." "I'm through with gossip." "I'll quit tomorrow."

If you are with me thus far, then we are ready to take the first step with Jesus. That step is to remember our story—where we come from, what our life experiences are and how we have arrived at this place in our lives.

WHY OUR STORY?

David Ackles sings that everybody has a story to tell. True. And, according to my friend Dr. Robbie Greaves, people go to professional counselors because they want at least one person to know their story. We are made for relationships; we long to be known.

Our lives are an unfolding story. As the least instinctive of God's creatures, we are dependent, growing and learning throughout our childhood, teen-aged and adult years. Apart from crying and sucking for food to end our hunger pangs, we learn almost everything. Our years to adulthood are filled with relationships and experiences that mold our sense of self. In our vulnerability, we also are subject to hurt, pain, loss and abuse.

Since we live in a fallen world, parents or others who raise us are subject to its effects. All our families are dysfunctional to some extent. Perfectionism, performance for acceptance, love withheld, random punishments, name-calling, outbursts of uncontrolled anger, shaming and broken promises leave us broken inside. Words can be devastating. "Sticks and stones will break my bones, but names can never hurt me" is a lie. Names do hurt: "wimp," "shorty," "geek," "bimbo," "nerd," "dummy" (and even "carrots" if the movie *Anne of Green Gables* is to be believed). Fear of failure or fear itself can leave us immobilized. Rejection can scar us for a lifetime. Abuse by older children or adults warps our sense of self. If we are born into alcoholic families, we may learn to cope with stress by drinking, just as our parents did. All of this can set us up for addictions. So remember your story. Reflect on your story. Learn to tell your story. Let me model this by telling you mine.

DISCOVERING MY STORY

I was first exposed to hard-core addiction on the streets of Hollywood in the late 1960s. As pastor to students at Hollywood Presbyterian Church, I spent my time on college campuses with sorority and fraternity types. Suddenly everything changed. Race riots in Watts (a section of Los Angeles); anti-Vietnam War protests; student strikes closing campuses; and sex, drugs and rock 'n' roll sent hordes of counterculture flower children to our community. I was forced to face this revolution. On our church campus we opened a coffeehouse called the Salt Company, and we hit the streets and beaches with the gospel. Here in Los Angeles I found addicts of all kinds. When we started our first "crash pads," they came to live with us.

One of my friends, Mark, used 14 barbiturates, or "reds," each day just to maintain his habit. When he wanted to really party, he took as many as 16 a day. He also had lumps in his arms from missing his veins during heroin injections. After he became a Christian, we took him to a cabin in the mountains so that he could experience withdrawal from his chemical dependency. In our ignorance, we threw him in harm's way. Stopping cold turkey caused a seizure. I found myself on the floor as he stopped breathing. His face turned blue. With panic and prayer, I dug my finger through his clenched jaw and pulled with all my might. His teeth cut me to the bone (the scar is still there), but he gasped in air—one of the most beautiful sounds I have ever heard. Quickly, we got him to the Los Angeles County Hospital

Psychiatric Ward where he was medically detoxed. (Years later he graduated from Fuller Theological Seminary's School of Psychology.) This was my raw introduction to addiction.

Back then, I saw addiction through a narrow lens. I thought it only had to do with alcohol or street drugs. This experience put me in touch with the law, probation officers, rehabilitation centers and hospital emergency units. It was all very scary, challenging and, in a not-so-odd way, invigorating and exciting. I never knew what the next day would hold, but I did know that some crisis would be waiting. This was a chance to grow in my faith; Jesus was the answer to all the destruction around me. It also was a door for me to feel significant, alive and even addicted to my own crisis ministry. I loved the adrenaline surges as I went into action. Those were heady days!

Years later, my wife, Kathryn, and I found ourselves living in La Jolla, a wealthy seaside community in the southernmost part of California. I had inherited a little Presbyterian church, and with time on my hands, I got to know kids in our area. A friend of mine introduced me to her brother, Mark, a new Christian. He was a brilliant, disheveled, rock 'n' roll musician, like the musicians I had known before in Hollywood. He had been addicted to heroin for years, surfed, played in bands, lived in New York and Hollywood, and now was radically converted to Christ. His healing had come during one night of prayer with his sister. He had suffered no withdrawals from heroin—a real miracle. Mark now had a local band, Jonny Kat. Through him I met his band mates and a horde of kids who followed them from gig to gig. As I became involved in their lives, I found the same chemical addictions that I had encountered on the streets of Hollywood years before. Here I was, 20 years later, in the same crises. Illegal drugs look for money, and kids in La Jolla have a lot of it.

During that time, I attended a leaders' camp for Young Life (the teenaged evangelical movement through which I had been converted years before). On Saturday afternoon, I found myself talking with a successful developer in La Jolla and a leader in his church. He casually remarked that his daughter was a sex and drug addict. Her pain had sent him and his wife to Al-Anon (recovery support for families of chemically dependent people). There he learned that he too was an addict. Unlike his daughter, he was addicted to work. In his job, as he put projects together, he would go through the planning and negotiating buildup. When he consummated the deal, that was his fix, his high. He would come down and then build up again for the next big deal. His addiction to work was no surprise, but he continued. His father also had been an addict—to the church. As a Baptist pastor, he had started congregations throughout the West, was never home and always obsessed about his mission. My friend concluded that his family had generations of addicts, only the objects of the addictions differed.

Finally, I was forced to face my addictions. I was forced to look back at my own story.

This sent my mind reeling. As I looked at La Jolla, I realized that I lived in a community of 28,000 addicts (the population at the time). Like their parents, a high percentage of kids were addicted to drugs, sex or power. I knew many fathers who got on planes and flew around the country each week, making deals, sitting on boards of corporations and returning on the weekends with the money to keep their lifestyle afloat. No wonder their wives felt abandoned and their children were lost. No wonder they used drugs, people and all kinds of other things to fill the emptiness inside.

When my thinking got this far, I was forced to ask the next question: If I live among a whole horde of addicts, am I the only one who has escaped? Am I the happy, healthy, free exception to the rule? Finally, I was forced to face my own addictions. I was forced to look back at my own story.

REVISITING THE PAST

I was born in 1937. I still remember my parents turning on the radio as the Japanese bombed Pearl Harbor. They knew that life would never be the same again. And it wasn't. Because of the War, my dad left when I was four and returned when I was nine. How does a four-year-old boy process this? Consciously, he doesn't. It was a serious blow. Looking back, I felt abandoned. I missed my dad during crucial growing-up years. He wasn't there to throw the football, teach me how to stand up to bullies or help me mold my sense of self. Years later I realized that because of my dad's absence, I had concluded that there would be no one to meet my needs. Besides, my mom taught me that my job was to meet other people's needs. I became good at it. Afraid of abandonment, I would do almost anything to keep people liking me. Having little self-validation, I found it in other people's approval. I became a good performer by using others to feel good about myself. Again and again, I became addicted to people, their opinions, their views of me and their acceptance. Psychologists call this codependency. As an alcoholic is addicted to alcohol, a codependent is addicted to people. For me, losing friends (especially girlfriends) was a death experience. I felt there was nothing left inside of me.

I became a Christian when I was a sophomore in high school. My father, an engineer, taught me, "A place for everything and everything in its place." He was busy ordering his world. My mother taught me, "Leave the world a little better than you found it." She was busy improving her world. I was supposed to order my world and improve it at the same time—quite a task! Then Jesus came into my life. I had a real, lasting born-again experience. I knew from that day forward that He was and is real. While He changed my heart, He didn't really change my inherited perception of reality. I still saw the world as an ordered place— needing a bit of tweaking. It was later, on the chaotic streets of Hollywood, that Jesus began to break up this assumption. As drugs rolled in, as addicts died, as civil unrest (virtually civil war, at times) exploded, my ordered world began to collapse. It had swung out of control, and I was along for the ride. But what about improving the world? As I looked substance abuse in the face, I saw the depths of evil and bondage. At people's deepest pain, there was no way I could leave them or their world "a little better than I found it." The old answers just didn't work anymore.

At the same time, the crisis of the '60s opened new opportunities for my self-validation. People were dying from drug overdoses, the sexual genie (the Pill) was out of the bottle and the lid of middle-class respectability was blown off. Not only did this fuel my addiction to people, but it also powered my addiction to work—in this case, ministry. I found my moment of fame and relished it, trying to fill the void inside.

Along with my addiction to people and ministry, I became addicted to crisis. It elevated my mood. It gave me a purpose larger than myself. It threw me into action (or, perhaps, reaction). I could problem solve, reach out to people and, again, receive the validation I so desperately needed. Under amazing stress, I lost sleep, had a hard time keeping physically fit and, still single, neglected myself for the sake of the cause. At the point of a nervous breakdown—my heartbeat irregular—my doctor ordered me out of town for a complete rest. Certainly I was addicted to my adrenaline. I was also addicted to caffeine and sugar. My drugs of choice were legal stimulants that kept me going.

Amid all of this, God used me (and began to break me). We were thrown into the Jesus movement and saw thousands come to Christ. We experienced the massive cultural changes that the Church had to address. We learned the power of the "simple" gospel again and again. Through our coffeehouse, we helped pioneer the changes in Christian music, which still affect the Church today. We learned in the raw the indispensable necessity of real Christian community. We also saw a large, established evangelical church rise to the occasion and not miss the moment as so many others did. God also changed me as my old assumptions no longer worked. This eventually opened the door to a whole new adventure with Christ and the power of His Spirit.

At the same time—and this is my point here—unresolved childhood issues caught up with me. I had used my position and people to meet my needs for validation and to build status. I had used the crisis to manage the loneliness, insecurity and fear of abandonment that lived inside of me. Success and approval had become idols. Who I knew in the larger evangelical world and my recognition there had given me identity and satisfaction. But all that was about to change.

As I have said, things were now out of control. Nothing really fit. There was no assurance that the world was better or that I was improving it. These "myths" now seemed daydreams of a bygone, exhausted era. One experience that helped destroy my previous perceptions of reality was when I met my first hippie, after preaching a summer morning service at Hollywood Presbyterian Church. Her name was Cheryl. She had come off the streets that Sunday in crisis, hoping to hide in the largest church she knew. But God had touched her, and she stood waiting for me as I shook hands at the door. After the sanctuary had emptied, we sat down in a pew.

Mascara streaked her face. Her story was simple. Her mom had thrown her out when she was 15. She had ended up on the Sunset Strip—the Los Angeles neighborhood of bars, clubs, coffeehouses, theaters and swirling mobs of teenagers in the mood to party or fight. Sleeping around, she had become pregnant, which had driven her to church. At the end of her story, Cheryl said, "I'm too bad for God to love me." I knew that she was not far from the Kingdom. In 20 minutes, the wait was over. Cheryl prayed and asked Jesus to forgive her and come into her life. Through her, the door into the hippie world cracked open for me.

The next Sunday, after teaching the college class, I found myself on the patio surrounded by students and adult leaders. Suddenly Cheryl appeared. She spotted me, let out a shriek, ran over, threw her arms around me and gave me a kiss, right on the lips. Every muscle in my body froze. My face flushed. As a single, careful young pastor, I felt like my head turned 360 degrees as I looked for elders.

Cheryl's behavior was out of order. But as I stood there frozen, Paul's word to the Galatians passed through my mind: "It is for freedom that Christ has set us free" (5:1). The thought hit me: *Who is really free here? Not me. I am consumed with the question, What would people think? While I feel out of control, maybe, just maybe, I am coming under control—the control of the Jesus who let a woman of the streets wash His feet with her tears.*

I was definitely on a new journey. My perceptions of reality were being shattered. My deep inner needs were being exposed. The losses of the past were catching up with me. And through it all, Jesus was there with me. As one world was falling away, a new one was being born—a world of healing, new life in the Spirit, freedom and of becoming truly human—the real journey of becoming more like Jesus.

These are parts of my story—and all the way it is a story with Jesus. He knew me when He formed me in my mother's womb. He chose my parents. He brought me to Himself and gradually shattered my childhood myths. He showed me my dysfunction, my family issues, my idols. He exposed a deep emptiness and loneliness inside. He released me (and continues to release me) from bondages, revealing more of His power and grace. He opened me up to a perception of reality that is more real, more satisfying and more practical than that which I inherited from my family.

DISCOVERING YOUR STORY

Jesus invites you to reflect back on your past, however painful it may be. He promises to be with you as you do so. He is the good physician. He only hurts to heal. As long as negative conditioning, losses, abuses and unhealthy ways of relieving pain drive you, you will never be the person He created you to be and to become. Remember, Jesus draws wounded people. He won't wound you. He is a "friend of . . . 'sinners'" (Matt. 11:19; Luke 7:34). As the totally whole, totally righteous Son of God, He attracts marginalized, broken, pain-filled people from every station, class and race. They come to Him in the Gospels and undress. They show Him their wounds: "Look, Jesus, at my leprosy" (see Matt. 8:2-3; Mark 1:40-42; Luke 5:12-13); "Jesus, I'm blind" (see Matt. 9:27-28; 20:30; Mark 8:22-23; 20:50-52); "Jesus, help this paralyzed man" (see Matt. 8:6-7; Mark 2:3-5; Luke 5:23-25); "Jesus, here is a woman bent over for 18 years" (see Luke 13:10-12); "Jesus, this woman was caught in the act of adultery. What about her?" (see John 8:3-4).

As people undress before the Lord, He loves them, forgives them, drives out their demons, heals them and restores their broken, fallen humanity. They are set free from their pasts. They walk away with new dignity, purpose and destiny. For them, His kingdom has come. They now know that Jesus eternally loves them. That is that.

Come to Jesus, and don't be afraid to "undress" before Him. As you do so, consider the following questions:

- In what kind of a family did you grow up?
- What was your relationship with your father?
- What was your relationship with your mother?
- Are you able to see your parents realistically and not idealize them?
- How did you relate to any brothers or sisters?
- What were the crises in your life growing up? How did you cope with them?
- Were you called names? Did they stick?
- When were you exposed to drugs, alcohol and nicotine? How did this affect you?
- When did you become sexually active (assuming you have become sexually active)? What were the consequences?
- How much of this have you shared with Jesus?
- How much of this have you shared with others you trust?
- What do you think Jesus' attitude toward this would be? (Read on!)
- Who were your role models? Who did you want to be like?
- What can you learn from all of this?

Take every pain, every sadness, every hurt and every loss to Jesus and surrender all to Him as best you can. And keep on doing it!

Define "Addiction" and Learn How It Works

"Addiction" is one of those slippery words smuggled into popular language and meaning any number of things. For example, in a current country-and-western song, a mesmerized lover sings about his "sweet addiction." Someone holding up a box of chocolates exclaims, "These are addicting." Formerly, to call someone an addict conjured up pictures of lonely men with shriveled bodies and bloodshot eyes, hugging dark streets; druggies dealing on blighted corners; junkies shooting up in hallways; or johns heading to red-light districts for quick sex. In light of this, how can Gerald May say, "We are all addicts in every sense of the word"?[1]

What Do We Mean by "Addiction"?

The Traditional View

Consider several perspectives. Dr. Drew Pinsky, cohost of MTV's *Loveline,* gives us the traditional view. He limits addiction to chemical abuse that usually needs medical detox (alcohol, illegal drugs, abused prescription drugs—but could include nicotine, weight-loss pills and so on). For him, "[Addiction is] the use of any potentially harmful substance with no therapeutic value that affects the brain."[2] It includes "the continued use of a substance in spite of its consequences."[3] The key symptom is compulsion. Pinsky writes, "Well, in reality, no matter what they acknowledge, addicts just can't stop. That is addiction—the inability to stop, no matter what. Addicts know every consequence of their addiction: lost jobs, screwed-up relationships, squandered money, betrayed relatives and so on. But they can't help their behavior."[4] Addiction has its roots in biology. It carries "the secret relationship between drugs, the brain, biology and disease."[5] This leads Pinsky to his comprehensive definition: "[Addiction is] a biological disorder with a genetic basis, plus progressive use in the face of adverse consequences, and denial of a problem."[6]

Like Pinsky, Dr. Ronald Ruden identifies addiction as the brain's "gotta have it" craving for chemicals. This comes from abnormal levels of brain substances designed to ensure our survival and well-being. For example, dopamine is the brain's accelerator and serotonin is its brake. When these neurochemicals are unbalanced, we are unbalanced. We are too "up" or too "down." Chemical abnormality keeps us in an activated survival mode, a state of stress. We feed our addictions as if our lives depend on it. Ruden defines addictive behavior "as the compulsive use of a substance or activity. 'Gotta have it' occurs because the brain produces a craving response for that substance or activity. No craving, no addictive behavior. No addictive behavior, no addiction."[7] He adds, "Obsessive thoughts, the inability to resist and the inability to stop, accompanied by feelings of powerlessness and inadequacy are the elements of individual stories of addiction, no matter what the substance or activity involved."[8] It is as if we are on the *Titanic,* scared witless, grabbing life jackets, finding they don't fit us and then, even more stressed, grabbing some more.

What we learn from Pinsky and Ruden is that addiction is a disease, not simply a moral failure or personality disorder. It starts with the brain. As a disease, it is treatable. Pinsky identifies addiction with chemical abuse. Ruden agrees and adds compulsive activities as well. But is brain chemistry the root of all addictions? Are we victims of biological determinism? No way! Continued trauma (like the loss of a parent), psychological dependency, chronic sexual stimulation, family alcoholism or spiritual abuse may lead to a craving brain. In such cases, the brain is not triggering the craving; rather, it is responding to the pain coming at it and is destabilized. If we look beyond our brain's chemistry, we see that many feel a deep spiritual emptiness and try to fill it with something or someone, which leads to addiction. Paul said, "Having lost all sensitivity, they have given themselves over to sensuality so as to indulge in every kind of impurity, with a continual lust for more" (Eph. 4:19).

The Codependent View

Melody Beattie describes addictions to people. In treating alcoholics, she realized that "the family is the patient."[9] If the alcoholic is addicted to alcohol, then the codependent is addicted to him or her. The famous example is the wife who finds her identity in her alcoholic husband. He gets sober. She divorces him and marries another alcoholic to restore her lost sense of self. Beattie admits that "codependency" is fuzzy, because it is a "gray, fuzzy condition."[10] Having said that, she goes on to define a codependent person as one who has "let another person's behavior affect him or her [adversely], and who is obsessed with controlling that person's behavior."[11] The word "obsessed" is key. The codependent defines himself or herself by that person. Judith MacNutt states: "As he is dying, someone else's life passes before him."[12] Anne Wilson Schaef claims that all in the helping professions (i.e., psychologists, social workers, pastors, youth workers) are untreated codependents.[13] For John Bradshaw, codependency is the "disease of today. All addictions are rooted in codependence, and codependence is a symptom of abandonment. We are codependents because we've lost ourselves." Bradshaw adds, "Codependence is a core addiction. It is a diseased form of life. Once a person believes that his identity lies outside himself in a substance, activity or another person, he has found a new god, sold his soul and become a slave."[14] I confess that this has been (and still can be) a major issue for me.

The Three-Pronged View: Biological, Psychological, Spiritual

While stress is one root of addiction, it is not the only one. Dr. Gerald May notes that for generations psychologists held that all self-defeating behavior was caused by repression. (For example, we repress our need to be loved out of our fear of being hurt.) But May now believes that addiction is "a separate and even more self-defeating force."[15] It abuses our freedom and makes us do the things we really don't want to do. If repression stifles desire, addiction attaches desire, and "bonds and enslaves the energy of desire to certain specific behaviors, things or people."[16] The result? "These objects of attachment then become preoccupations and obsessions. They come to rule our lives."[17] May writes,

> I am not being flippant when I say that all of us suffer from addiction. Nor am I reducing the meaning of addiction. I mean in all truth that the psychological, neurological and spiritual dynamics of full-fledged addiction are actively at work within every human being. The same processes that are responsible for addiction to alcohol and narcotics are also responsible for addiction to ideas, work, relationships, power, moods, fantasies and an endless variety of other things. We are all addicts in every sense of the word. Moreover, our addictions are our own worst enemies. They enslave us with chains that are of our own making and yet that, paradoxically, are virtually beyond our control. Addiction also makes idolaters of us all, because it forces us to worship these objects of attachment, thereby preventing us from truly, freely loving God and one another. . . . Yet . . . our addictions can lead us to a deep appreciation of grace. They can bring us to our knees.[18]

For May, addiction has biological, psychological and spiritual components. Along with disordered brain functions, addictions serve to medicate childhood wounds and alter our moods. As we become dependent on them, they become idols in our lives. May concludes, "Addiction is the most powerful psychic enemy of humanity's desire for God."[19] For him, addiction is desire gone amuck. Rather than being nailed to God, it is nailed to other gods. They become the functional objects of our worship. When desire is freed to love God, healing comes, and we become human again.

The Spiritual View

Finally, there is a spiritual base to all addictions. If we do not worship the living God, we will worship someone or something else. Compulsivity is not simply biologically or psychologically driven; it is a spiritual issue. As Blaise Pascal is known to have said, we all have a God-shaped vacuum that He alone can fill. Stuffing chemicals or passions or people into it will never ultimately satisfy. The Bible says we become like what we worship: "[The Hebrews] followed worthless idols and became worthless

> *If we do not worship the living God, we will worship someone or something else.*

themselves" (Jer. 2:5). "But when they came to Baal Peor, they consecrated themselves to that shameful idol [fertility cult] and became as vile as the thing they loved" (Hos. 9:10). Worship sex, become a lustful person. Worship money, become a greedy person. Worship drugs, become a chemically dependent person. Worship yourself, become a narcissistic person.

As Tom Wright says, an idol is, first of all, a perversion of God's good creation.[20] Sex is good. Sexual abuse, pornography, incest, adultery and deviancy pervert it.[21] Chemicals are good. Drug abuse perverts them. Love of country is good. Fanatical patriotism—"my country right or wrong"—perverts it.

Second, idols make us feel 10-feet tall. They enhance our lives. A sexual predator seduces women and feels invincible and alive. A wallflower does a few lines of coke and is the life of the party. A student joins a pro-gay or peace movement and feels powerful and important for the first time.

Third, idols demand sacrifice. We offer them our time and money. Little by little, we give up our freedom, individuality, family, friends, honesty, present and future.

Fourth, we justify our idols philosophically. Hugh Hefner blatantly set out to create an empire built on liberating male lust. To do so he buried himself in the Playboy mansion in Chicago and wrote his "Playboy Philosophy," a dull, rambling, shallow justification for his assault on traditional morality. The drug culture creates its own ideological defense of addiction and tries to take down a generation with it. The legalization of street drugs is continually justified by political, economic, legal and medical arguments.

Fifth, our idols finally kill us. We think we have captured them; they capture us. We think we possess them; they possess us. Sexual liberation breeds sexual addiction, abortions and venereal diseases with AIDS as the extreme outcome. Street drugs breed addiction, gangs, violence and huge criminal cartels that corrupt whole cities and even countries.

There is a way that seems right to a man, but in the end it leads to death (Prov. 14:12).

In summary, addiction is a complex spiritual, psychological and biological craving for something or someone, often running in cycles, leading to compulsivity, powerlessness and bondage. It destroys our freedom, dignity and humanity. It results in "death" in life.

WHAT ARE THE SYMPTOMS OF ADDICTION?

Addiction is identified by the three Cs: (1) craving; (2) control loss; (3) continued use. Let's look at each one.

Craving

First, craving sets in. Let's suppose that when you were a child your mama would tell you that she loved you and then would hand you a piece of chocolate cake. As a result, you now identify chocolate cake with your mother's love. Years later, you find yourself on a Friday night watching TV, depressed and lonely. You remember how much your mother loves you. You get a warm feeling. Then you remember that you have a chocolate cake in the refrigerator. A piece would taste good, and you would feel mama's love once again. So you cut a slice and pour a glass of milk. Settling back in front of the TV, you enjoy the cake. The sugar speeds up your heart rate and elevates your mood. Now you really feel loved. But as you come off the sugar rush, you experience the "sugar blues" and sink back into depression.

Control Loss

Second, you remember that there is still more cake to be eaten. Craving turns into control loss. You go back to the refrigerator and cut yourself a larger piece. Again, the sugar elevates your mood, but the depression that follows is deeper. Soon you are rushing to the refrigerator, grabbing the cake and stuffing it into your mouth. You are out of control.

Continued Use

Third, control loss leads to continued use. Now you hide chocolate cakes in your closet, in your glove compartment, under the bed. You also know every bakery in town. You know all the kinds of chocolate cake they make: German chocolate, devil's food, double-trouble chocolate. You not only continue to use chocolate cake, but you also know your "dealers." You maintain your sources of supply. Your craving has led to control loss and now is fixed by continued use. You are a chocoholic.

WHAT IS THE ADDICTION CYCLE?

Ronald Ruden writes, "No craving, no addictive behavior."[22] While this is true, it does not mean that without the behavior there is no addiction. Craving is not necessarily constant; triggers can set it off. The resulting behavior often runs in cycles. First, there is the pain (craving) that produces the build-up phase. Stress begins to mount. It may be a craving for food or safety, an anxiety attack or lust. It may be an obsession to see a person on whom we are dependent. It may be an overwhelming sense of emptiness that demands to be filled or a fear that needs to be numbed.

The buildup then leads to the compensatory behavior phase—the addictive act. This may be bingeing with food, picking up a prostitute, going on a "drunk," getting loaded for the weekend, hooking up with an old lover, closing a business deal, masturbating or going on a shopping spree.

The compensatory behavior then leads to the relief phase. We come down. The stress or craving has been satisfied—for the moment. We feel peace, release. But getting loaded for the weekend, picking up a one-night stand or whatever else our drug of choice may be brings on the crash. We are filled with guilt and remorse. We have violated our conscience and sullied our relationship with God. We hate ourselves even more. We now enter the consequence phase, which is characterized by more guilt and shame. Not only does the craving return, but it is also now more intense (this disease is progressive). We return to the build-up phase. The pain, now deeper (if we are not rationalizing or in denial), drives us toward acting out again. The cycle is a downward spiral. We are driven deeper and deeper into our addiction with only moments of relief. As Paul admits, "I do not understand what I do. For what I want to do I do not do, but what I hate I do" (Rom. 7:15). We also can echo his cry, "What a wretched man I am! Who will rescue me from this body of death?" (v. 24).

How Do You Understand Addiction?

Step 2, then, is to define "addiction" and know how it works. We need to identify our cravings and the cycles that run in us. Reflect on the definitions discussed in this chapter and try to write your own definition. The following questions and action points should help you.

- What definitions of "addiction" make sense to you?
- Where do you find echoes in your own experience?
- Where does stress or craving appear in your life?
- What triggers your craving?
- What or who are the idols in your life?
- How do they function?
- What are your symptoms of addiction?
- Can you give a personal example of how the addiction cycle works in your life?
- How do you get relief?
- Ask Jesus to break through any denial.
- Ask Him to take away the fear of facing the truth.
- Ask Him to give you hope for freedom.

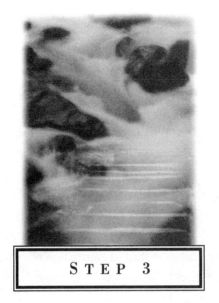

Get to the Causes of Addiction

While we have seen that addiction affects us biologically, psychologically and spiritually, we need to look at its causes more closely. Knowing the causes throws light on our cravings and how we act out. Following the lead of Pinsky, Ruden and May, we start with the brain.

GOD'S GOOD BRAIN

The brain is God's greatest natural gift to each one of us. It is our conductor, arranging and directing the harmonious functions of our glands, organs, nervous system and body parts. It is our computer, storing the memories and learning of a lifetime, allowing us to access them as wanted or needed. It is our chief operating officer, commanding and relaying our emotions, actions and reactions. It is our security guard, automatically protecting us in excessive heat or cold and defending us against shock or violence. Most important, it is the vehicle of our soul, the instrument of our personality. For Christians, our regenerated spirit expresses itself through our brain and exits it at death. What then can we learn about the brain from the creation story? Genesis 1:27-28 teaches that God made us in His image for relationship and rulership (stewardship, or "dominion," v. 28, *NKJV*) over His world. We are to be the agents of His reign on this planet. Through our creation, He gives us basic instincts for survival and growth. In our brain's core, we are driven to eat rather than be eaten and to reproduce the race.

Basic Instinct 1: Eat

Our first instinct, then, is to eat. When hunger stresses us, we satisfy its demands. This is God's gift—a feast of vegetation:

> Then God said, "Behold, I have given you every plant yielding seed that is on the surface of all the earth, and every tree which has fruit yielding seed; it shall be food for you" (v. 29, *NASB*).

Our need to eat also represents our need for nurture and for physical and spiritual growth.

Basic Instinct 2: Don't Be Eaten

Our second instinct is not to be eaten. It is the need for security, protection and well-being—the "herd instinct." We see this need met in the animal kingdom when members of the same species live together. In the herd, they are emotionally and physically safe. Likewise, we are social beings, created for relationships with God and with each other. We need to feel safe in a family, tribe, community and nation. Loneliness is not good. The first negative in the Bible appears in the midst of God's good creation: "The LORD God said, 'It is not good for the man to be alone. I will make a helper suitable for him'" (2:18). This basic need drives us to seek companionship. We long for love and intimacy. When Eve is brought to Adam, he sings out, "This is now bone of my bones and flesh of my flesh" (v. 23). While this desire for relationship came before sin entered the world, after sin's intrusion, our need for protection and security has become all the greater. The stress of loneliness and the fear of assault, natural disaster, disease and death all drive us to care for each other.

Basic Instinct 3: Reproduce
Our third instinct is to reproduce. Sex is a powerful drive. It is intimately related to the drives for food (life) and security (community). God blesses us as sexual beings. He wants our race to continue through the generations. As the creator, He gives us the ability to procreate: "God blessed them; and God said to them, 'Be fruitful and multiply, and fill the earth'" (1:28, *NASB*). But God also channels this powerful drive. He creates us for permanent ("For this reason a man will leave his father and mother"), heterosexual ("and be united to his wife"), monogamous ("and they will become one flesh") relationships (2:24). Sexual union is more than a physical act. It is also the spiritual union of two persons. The result—before sin came into the world—is shame-free living: "And the man and his wife were both naked and were not ashamed" (v. 25, *NASB*).

As sexual beings we have the joy of joining in the creator's continuing creation—holding a newborn in our arms and seeing that person become all that God made him or her to be. Beyond our overt sexuality, the passion and creativity in our lives are all extensions of this creative urge. All fruitfulness is a sign of God's blessing.

GOD'S GOOD BRAIN CORRUPTED

As we have seen, we are all born with the basic instincts for food, security and sexual union. They lie deep in the core of our brains. But Satan led a revolt in heaven, which stained Earth. Disguised as a serpent, he tempted our first parents to assert their independence from God, violate the limitation He placed on their lives and become their own gods instead. By their sin, Adam and Eve corrupted the goodness of their creation, shaking the earth to its foundation and inflecting all of humanity.

We now live outside of Eden—God's idyllic garden where our instincts were to be fulfilled in wonderful, natural, perfect ways. Damaged by the Fall (the rebellion against our original state), we are unconsciously set up for addiction. As Pinsky writes, "More recent findings have focused on the relationship between addiction and the drives in the deepest brain structures that are outside of conscious volitional control."[1] He continues by informing us that the chemically addicted suffer from a disorder in the drive centers of the brain: "specifically the so-called mesolimbic reward center . . . that part of the brain [that] . . . doesn't have language or logic. . . . It exists merely to increase the drive that activates behavior, fostering survival. It's the survival center, and it's gone awry."[2]

Infected Genes

The first consequence of the Fall, then, is that our brains have been corrupted. We inherit genes infected by sin. We have brains that are "out of order." Our instincts for food, security and reproduction often malfunction, not by our own choice, but by our inheritance. We are conceived from a damaged gene pool and carry the effects for a lifetime. The delicate hormonal balance in our brains, for many, is broken. We release too much dopamine, which revs us up, or too little serotonin, which calms us down. This can predispose us to continual craving. We often carry false shame and guilt over our genetic inheritance: *If I just trusted God, this depression would go. If I knew Jesus' peace, my anxiety would lift.* Perhaps—and perhaps not. We come into the world as damaged goods. We all need more than faith, or moral resolve. We often need Jesus to heal us from past wounds outside of our consciousness or control.

A Rebellious World

The second consequence of the Fall is that we live in an imperfect world. It is a world in rebellion against God and dominated by the devil. This means that from birth on our brains grow and develop under different kinds of pressures, stresses and assaults. Made in God's image (see Gen. 1:26), we are the least instinctual of all His creatures. Most of our behaviors are learned. Although our gender identity is inherent in our sexual design, we learn that we are male or female through social conditioning. In Ruden's metaphor, our brains are like the seashore, landscaped by tides, winds and storms.[3]

Childhood abuse is one storm that damages our brain's functions. We may rationalize the abuse—*It's my fault my father raped me*—or block it out for survival. Still, we have been landscaped for life. Childhood loss is another storm. Divorce, death of a parent or long-term illness in the family also landscapes our brains. These hurts and wounds may take on a life of their own and affect how the brain secretes its hormones. Pinsky wrote, "The difficult part is the unexpressed pain that's buried far beneath the surface, the original hurt around which everything else is structured [even including the way our brain functions]."[4]

Mental illness, acute anxiety, depression and a host of other illnesses often result.

Our brain also is landscaped by puberty. The hormonal surges of testosterone or estrogen make our brains sexually mature and our bodies ready to reproduce. This creates emotional stress for teenagers. As I heard Dr. James Dobson say on a Focus on the Family radio broadcast, "You can't heal or exorcise adolescence; you just have to get through it (and we all do)." In this period of life, if we bombard the brain with chemicals such as alcohol, narcotics or nicotine, or induce repeated pornographic images, its landscape will be permanently altered. This may leave the brain addicted for a lifetime. As a result, our society enacts laws to try to protect minors against such assaults. Tragically, much of the advertising of the beverage, tobacco and pornographic industries is aimed at adolescents.

Additionally, our brains are landscaped throughout a lifetime. We continue to grow, adjust and change depending on the input coming into our consciousness. The instinct to eat can become a monster of obesity, anorexia or bulimia. Overeating may protect our fragile egos with fat. Sculpting a prepubescent body by purging may help us fend off sexual predators. The herd instinct may find us in the wrong herd. The need for security may lead us into destructive, controlling, abusive relationships. Rather than protected by our own, we discover we are zebras in a pride of lions. The instinct for reproduction may turn us into sex addicts always on the make, searching for the next sexual high, never satisfied.

Does this analysis leave us frustrated or despondent? We must not let it. Whatever we have inherited, experienced or welcomed into our brains, however they have been landscaped, Jesus can and does heal it. He offers us the power of His Spirit and a healing community for our recovery (which often includes therapists and medical doctors). After all, He came not for the well but for the sick. As Pinsky says of recovery, "We're talking about rewiring your brain."[5]

Besides the corruption of the instincts to eat, to not be eaten and to reproduce, which was brought about by the Fall, what else sets us up for addictions?

PLEASURE AND PAIN

We are created to seek pleasure and avoid pain. At a base level this is part of our survival instinct. But it is also much more. God has created us for pleasure—His and ours. He has given us the capacity to enjoy color, dimension, tastes, smells, sounds, touch, sexual stimulation and release. More deeply still, He has created us for joy.

> *God has created us for pleasure; He has created us for joy.*

Normally we avoid pain, but we return again and again to pleasure. We seek to repeat enjoyable experiences and to keep satisfying relationships. At the same time, we quickly reach tolerance to any stimulant. One cup of coffee may wake us up now, but soon we will need two for the same effect. Since the chemistry of our bodies adjusts to our caffeine intake, we will need to increase the dosage. A short workout may release pleasurable endorphins, but soon we will need more exercise for a similar release. Seeking pleasure and needing more of the same are a setup for addiction. Also, if we use alcohol or drugs to numb the pain or overcome anxiety or shyness, when we reach tolerance, we will increase our usage. Somewhere, as our tolerance builds, we often cross the line into addiction.

DEPENDENCY

Normal human growth is from childhood dependency to adult interdependency. Many never make it. They live their adult lives dependent on people, substances or activities. Dr. Stanton Peele wrote that chemical addicts are fearful people with unmet dependency needs. He continued, "Disbelieving his own adequacy, recoiling from challenge, the addict welcomes control from outside himself as the ideal state of affairs."[6] Out of insecurity, these addicts fail to act; they simply react. They are happy when others are in control, although they may secretly resent them for it. They suffer from little sense of self or self-worth. They are people pleasers. Again, this opens them up for addiction. They easily become dependent on chemicals or other people to compensate for their inadequacy or emptiness.

FAMILY ABUSE

As we have seen, childhood abuse landscapes the brain. Sharon Wegscheider-Cruse claims that 96 percent of us come from dysfunctional families in which such abuse has happened.[7] (Because this is a fallen world, the number is really 100 percent.) In other words, we all come from families that fail to function according to God's design. One result is that over 75 million of us are touched directly by the disease of alcoholism alone.[8] Eighty-two percent of nurses are the oldest child of an alcoholic parent. (They learned early to become caregivers.)[9] Around 60 percent of all women and 50 percent of all men have eating disorders. As a result, they produce millions of underexercised and overweight children.[10]

Moreover, 50 percent of all children today will grow up in single-parent families that lack any permanent male influence. Referencing David Blankenhorn's phrase, this makes two cultures: the fathered and the fatherless.[11] Since the father's first responsibility is to protect the family, his absence leaves children open to every kind of abuse. Blankenhorn wrote:

Fatherlessness is the most harmful demographic trend of this generation. It is the leading cause of declining child well-being in our society. It is also the engine driving our most urgent social problems, from crime to adolescent pregnancy to child sexual abuse to domestic violence against women.[12]

Alice Miller observes that most of us have been set up for addiction by the verbal, physical or sexual abuse we experienced as children. As a result, we become detached from our feelings. We've been called names like "dumb," "stupid," "ugly" or "fat." We've been hit and spanked. In her words, we are "decent people once beaten."[13] Many of us have been sexually assaulted and molested. Mic Hunter described the consequences of boys' sexual abuse:

They will be damaged physically, emotionally, mentally and spiritually. Every aspect of their lives will be affected. When they become adults they will be plagued with sexual dysfunctions, troubled relationships, a poor sense of self-worth, and intimacy difficulties. Many will become drug addicts. Some will destroy themselves.[14]

Miller holds that if we've been raised in families in which we've been emotionally shut down, we will feel empty because of repressed childhood feelings, including a sense of powerlessness, personal violation and ungrieved childhood losses. Children's silence has been justified by what Miller calls "poisonous pedagogy,"[15] a misinterpretation of the fourth commandment to "honor your father and your mother" (Exod. 20:12; Deut. 5:16). Many have taken this to mean unquestioned submission from a weak and fearful child. Miller wrote, "If he is prevented from reacting in his own way, because the parents cannot tolerate his reactions (crying, sadness, rage) and forbid them . . . then the child will learn to be silent."[16] This emotional shutdown is the root of a disintegrated personality. The destruction of the child's inner life results in "the psychic murder of the child."[17]

These early humiliations are then transmitted to the next generation. Miller noted, "We punish our children for the arbitrary actions of our parents that we were not able to defend ourselves against. . . . The more we idealize the past . . . and refuse to acknowledge our childhood sufferings, the more we pass them on unconsciously to the next generation."[18] She continues, "Psychoses, drug addiction, and criminality are encoded expressions of these experiences."[19] As we have seen, abuse landscapes the brain. Virtually all of us experienced some violation in childhood, and our brain wiring and memories carry the consequences.

We have what John Bradshaw calls "the hole in the soul."[20] We try to fill this emptiness with all kinds of things: chemicals, food, gambling, exercise, work and relationships. But it only gets larger. However, there is an alternative. Rather than seeking to fill the hole and medicate the pain, we need to let Jesus heal us.

FACE THE CAUSES OF YOUR PAIN

Like mine, your brain comes with a genetic inheritance and has been landscaped by your life experiences. Now is a good time to take a second look at your own story. Again, get out of denial.

Your love for your parents need not protect you from the truth of your upbringing. Remember, apart from Jesus' healing in their lives, they mostly passed on to you what they had received from their parents. This will allow you to have grace toward them and toward yourself. Here are some questions to ask yourself:

- How has my need for nurture affected my life?
- How has my need for belonging and security affected my life?
- How has my sexual drive affected my life?
- What experiences through the years have landscaped my brain?
- How has my drive for pleasure set me up for addictions? What kinds?
- How have my dependency needs been met?
- Was I ever physically abused as a child?
- Was I ever verbally abused as a child?
- Was I ever sexually abused as a child?
- Which areas of pain am I medicating?
- What do I now need to give to Jesus?

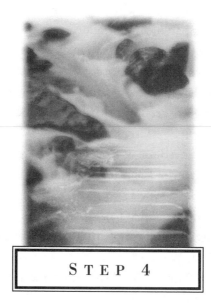

Get to the Root of Addiction

Why do so many people come to Christ and not get better? There are a number of reasons. First, Jesus strips away their defenses. They must face reality for the first time. The old adjustments and addictions no longer work. Along with receiving a new joy, they may also grieve losing their old ways of coping or their old relationships. Second, follow-up is often inadequate. They fail to find an authentic, caring community. Third, spiritual warfare comes against them. Fourth, they may still be in denial about the wounds from the past and the cravings of the present.

Even after breaking through denial, why are so many Christians still sick, trapped in compulsive behaviors? A key reason: Shallow diagnosis equals shallow cure. Most of us have heard the gospel in a simplistic way. The stress is laid on our decision for Christ. The preacher asks, "What would happen if you left here tonight and were killed in a head-on collision? Would you go to heaven or hell? The answer is in your hands. Your eternal destiny is at stake. I want you to get up out of your seat and come to Christ now." All the emphasis is on me and what I must do: I have to come forward. I have to decide. My choice determines my destiny. It is almost as if I were saving myself.

Such evangelism appeals to our sense of personal responsibility and our free choice. The message is that as an isolated individual, I have separated myself from God. Therefore, I have to repent and accept Jesus as my personal Savior. The focus is not on what God has done and is doing but on what I must do. This perpetuates the illusion that I am still in control. Everything rests on me.

Certainly we are morally responsible to become Christians. Yet our own sins and our decision for Christ are only part of the truth. I also have inherited a sinful nature, continually nurtured by the fallen world around me.

Simply focusing on our personal sin masks its depth. We miss radical evil and radical grace. If we think that we have a skin infection rather than cancer, we will settle for salve rather than surgery. Most Christians have settled for the salve of free will in order to explain their deepest problems: bondage, craving and compulsivity. We are satisfied, in Dallas Willard's phrase, with "sin management."[1] But what does the Bible really teach?

THE BIBLICAL DIAGNOSIS

God's Word gives a profound picture of our condition:

As for you, you were dead in your transgressions and
sins, in which you used to live when you followed the
ways of this world and of the ruler of the kingdom of the
air [the prince of the power of the air, *RSV*], the spirit
who is now at work in those who are disobedient. All of
us also lived among them at one time, gratifying the
cravings of our sinful nature and following its desires
and thoughts. Like the rest, we were by nature objects of
wrath (Eph. 2:1-3).

Here, Paul addresses our fivefold problem. First, we are spiritually dead in transgressions and sins. Second, we follow the ways
of this fallen world. Third, the devil—"the ruler of the kingdom of
the air" or "the prince of the power of the air"—dominates us.
Fourth, we gratify the cravings of our sinful nature, its desires and
thoughts. Fifth, we are the objects of God's wrath. God says no to
our total corruption.

Problem 1: We Are Spiritually Dead in Transgressions and Sins
First, then, we all suffer from *generational sin*. From birth there is a
hole in the soul, making our lives unmanageable. "In sin did my
mother conceive me" (Ps. 51:5, *KJV*), King David writes. Similarly,
in his song "Saved," Bob Dylan acknowledges that he was "blind-
ed by the devil, born already ruined" when he came out of the
womb.[2]

From Adam and Eve to the present, we have inherited a chain of
sin. Our family tree is dysfunctional. Since generational sin
becomes progressively worse, we are the victims of accumulated
abuse. As Paul said in Romans 5:20, "sin abounded" (*KJV*). Alcoholic
parents raise alcoholic children. The abused become abusers. The
cycle goes on and grows throughout the human bloodline.

We are not only addicts but also idolaters in every sense of
the word. Our craving brain is predisposed to self-consumption

(rather than nurture), isolation or control (rather than serenity in community) and lust (rather than faithfulness in marriage). Because we are spiritually dead, we cannot save ourselves. We need a Savior to raise the dead! We only come alive through the powerful, creative Word of Christ, calling us out of our tombs. We must be reborn by the Spirit of God. He convicts us of our need for Christ and regenerates us. We respond to His initiative. This is all by His grace alone, so no one can boast (see Eph. 2:8-9). Our forgiveness, our freedom, our healing and our future are in His hands. We are completely dependent on Him.

Problem 2: We Follow the Ways of this Fallen World

Second, we are subject to *environmental sin*. We conform to the "ways of this world." Although blessed by God's providential care, we live in a culture separated from Him. Only this explains the evil we face. Moreover, the world constantly reinforces our own struggles with addiction. Advertising drives consumerism. It tells us how inadequate we are. We have the wrong look, the wrong smell, the wrong car, the wrong beverage. A lot of this is subtle, but the message is clear. The media that promises to redeem our unhappiness, insecurity and loneliness by consumption meets our craving brain. It will fulfill the very cravings that it continually stimulates.

Dr. Drew Pinsky, cohost of MTV's *Loveline*, offered this penetrating critique of the culture:

> I have plenty of reasons to call the culture up on charges.
> . . . The culture is like a living, breathing beast that feeds its own need to exist and grow at the expense of the individual. Our world is full of people with narcissistic problems who look to escape those feelings and be gratified—and the culture steps right in to meet those needs. Many of those contributing to the culture are sick themselves.

It doesn't take a shrink to count the number of celebrities who end up in rehab, get into fights, or pose for mug shots. The media has become an instant-response machine, ratcheting our tolerance ever upward in cycles of arousal and gratification. All of this can be arresting, fun, sexy, most of all, it sells, but it doesn't heal.[3]

Pinsky added:

Our culture is just like the junk food we live on. It fills you up without the distracting burden of nourishment. An average person exposed to television, movies, and magazines is overwhelmed by messages that arouse, stimulate, and suggest that the answer to all problems is the same, gratification. Have a beer, take a pill, roll on the deodorant, get a Whopper, JUST DO IT! These are just diversions from an empty world. If you've been abused, if you don't know how to trust, and if you're already overwhelmed by feelings you can't handle, an icy six-pack won't solve anything. Nor will a new pair of Nikes. Nor will ninety-nine new ways to drive your man wild in bed, as all the women's magazines promise. They aggravate the stimulation. They ignore the problem.[4]

Consider Pinsky's description of the media: "an instant-response machine, ratcheting our tolerance ever upward in cycles of arousal and gratification." In other words, the media drives us deeper and deeper into bondage and addiction, and ironically, the strength of our economy depends on these cycles to promote consumer spending.

Problem 3: The Devil Dominates Us
Third, we are *dominated by the devil*, subject to demonic hordes

ruled by "the ruler of the kingdom of the air." The devil attacks like a stealth bomber, slipping past our natural defenses to destroy us. We live in the illusion that we are in control, but we are really out of control, or under demonic control. Our emotional shutdown and our addictive cravings may be inherited, but they are reinforced by the spiritual oppression around us. Satan's purpose is clear—he stirs our rebellion against God and holds us in disobedience. If this is true (and it is), then a simple appeal to addicts to "get over it" is in vain. Spiritual forces must be defeated with spiritual weapons. The good news is that Jesus has disarmed them on the cross, fulfilling the demands of the law and stripping these demons of their weapons of performance anxiety, guilt and condemnation (see Col. 2:13-15). Our freedom includes liberation from these dark powers.

Problem 4: We Gratify the Cravings of Our Sinful Nature, Its Desires and Thoughts

Fourth, we contribute to the immense evil in us and around us by our own personal sin. We choose to live in the cravings of our bodies and minds. We are not only caught in sin, but we also like it. Paul wrote:

> Although they know God's righteous decree that those who do such things [envy, murder, strife, deceit and so on] deserve death, they not only continue to do these very things but also approve of those who practice them (Rom. 1:32).

We add our hearty approval to the sin that we are born into. Usually, unconsciously, we ally ourselves with the powers of darkness. But we cannot shrink from our moral responsibility. All of us have made our own contribution.

In light of this, we must ask ourselves, *What is my core problem? What is the basis for this severe diagnosis?* This takes us back to creation.

Problem 5: God Says No to Our Total Corruption

As we have already seen, Genesis 1 shows us that we have been made in the image of God, male and female, and given dominion over the planet. Genesis 2 reveals that we have been made for each other. The final verse of this chapter describes our ideal state. Adam and Eve were "naked and were not ashamed" (v. 25, *NASB*). That is, they were totally vulnerable, free and transparent, in complete communion with God and with each other. There was no shame base to their lives.

In Genesis 3, however, sin quickly enters paradise. Our original parents fall for Satan's temptation to run their own lives—"be like God" (v. 5). Pride promises that they can live independently, in control of everything. But after their rebellion, rather than knowing everything—as Satan had promised they would—they simply know that they are naked. Filled with shame, they go into hiding. Separated from each other, they cover their nakedness with aprons. Separated from God, they jump into the bushes.

As Adam and Eve abandon God, God abandons them. They die spiritually, stand under His judgments and will eventually die physically. This is His no to them and to their sin. There is no more devastating an experience than this total rejection. It is death in life, which brings loneliness, insecurity, fear and self-hatred.

SHAME

The result of total rejection—death in life—is a deep wound in the soul. I refer to this wound as a "being wound," which is the source for our shame-based lives. Shame lies at the root of our addictions; it is the hole in the soul.

So what is shame? Gershen Kaufman answered:

[Shame] is the most poignant experience of the self by the self whether felt in humiliation or cowardice or in a sense of failure to cope successfully with challenge. Shame is a wound felt on the inside, dividing us both from ourselves and from one another.[5]

John Bradshaw added:

[Toxic shame] is the source of most of the disturbing inner states that deny full human life. Depression, alienation, self-doubt, isolating loneliness, paranoid and schizoid phenomena, compulsive disorder, splitting of the self, perfectionism, a deep sense of inferiority, inadequacy or failure, the so-called borderline conditions, and disorders of narcissism all result from shame. Shame is a kind of soul murder. Once shame is internalized, it is characterized by a kind of psychic numbness that becomes the foundation for a kind of death in life. Forged in the matrix of our source [family] relationships, shame conditions every other relationship in our lives. Shame is total non-acceptance.[6]

In other words, shame has to do with who we are at the deepest level—and it differs greatly from the feeling of guilt. Guilt says I've done something wrong; shame says there is something wrong with me. Guilt says I've made a mistake; shame says I am a mistake. Guilt says what I did was not good; shame says I *am* no good.[7]

Shame is then reinforced down through the generations. When we hear our parents' pronouncements such as, "I'm ashamed of *you*," the meaning is not "I'm ashamed of what you've *done*," but "I'm ashamed of who you *are*." Many of us have heard, "You ought to be ashamed of yourself." This exhortation to shame focuses not on our action but on our being—ourselves! Here the consequences of the Fall are reinforced. Shame penetrates deeper and deeper, and we become ashamed of shame.

As we have seen, when we abandon God, He abandons us. God's love is holy love. It cannot tolerate sin. Because He respects our being (as we are made in His image), He honors our

> *Without God we are a flash of consciousness in an empty, impersonal eternity.*

decision to live without Him—He will not drag us kicking and screaming into heaven. In despair, we find that without Him there is nothing at the core of our being; we are a flash of consciousness in an empty, impersonal eternity.

Although New Age religion encourages us to find the god within by altering our consciousness, we remain lonely, because the god within is still us. A musician friend of mine was told to look within himself for God. He looked and reported, "I found that there was nothing there." He quickly accepted Christ and added, "Now something is there."

Our response to this "hole" is shame. We cover up for fear of exposure. We hide the results of abandonment: depression, aching loneliness and the loss of our true selves. In the absence of God's image in us, we create false images, Hollywood movie sets behind which we hide. Our masks are made from our fears and fantasies. We play out the scripts written for us by other people; we act in someone else's movie. We become people pleasers, trapped by performance for acceptance. Or we choose to isolate in pride and anger instead.

By creating our cover-ups, we pass the buck. After the Fall, when God asked Adam and Eve how they knew they were naked, they immediately played the blame game. Adam replied, "The woman"; Eve joined, "The serpent" (Gen. 3:12-13). Here is the original dysfunctional family. Their addictive, codependent behavior rationalizes and avoids responsibility.

A NEW TESTAMENT UPDATE

Paul describes this shame-based, false self as life in the "flesh" (*NASB*) or the "sinful nature" (Rom. 7:18). When we live this way, we carry the illusion of our independence; we rely on ourselves rather than on God. Narcissism and pride drive us; we think we are in control.

The classic expression of the false self, or life in the flesh, appears in Romans 7:14. Here Paul described himself as "unspiritual," or "of flesh" (*NASB*), "sold as a slave to sin." Sin is not simply moral failure. It is a power that holds him captive. It is an addiction that he can't lick alone. Later, in verse 18, he confessed, "I know that nothing good lives in me, that is, in my sinful nature [flesh]." Here Paul makes an important qualification: His flesh is his false self. It is in opposition to his true being—the "me" created by God.

To be in the flesh is to be under sin's power and to define ourselves by our addictions. Gerald May says that we even become addicted to our "self-representational system," namely, the way we view ourselves in our various roles as father, mother, husband, wife and so on.[8] As we become attached to these self-images, they begin to control us. We are defined by what we do rather than by who we are.

To live in the flesh, then, is to live addictive lives. This is our fallen nature. We use our false selves to cover the hole in the soul.

Where do we go from here? The good news Jesus brings is that His heavenly Father is home waiting for us. Therefore, we need to get up in all our fear, pain and presumption and make the journey back to the Father's house. Only this will fill the hole in the soul.

LOOK AT THE ROOT OF ADDICTION IN YOUR LIFE

Behind all the cover-up, there is your relationship with God. Only as you see yourself in Him will life change for you. As you think through the spiritual basis for addictions, consider the following:

- Why do you think so many Christians come to Christ but don't get better?
- How do you understand your spiritual diagnosis for which Christ is the cure?
- In what ways have you experienced generational sin? What has been passed on to you from your family?
- In what ways have you experienced environmental sin? How has the world corrupted you?
- In what areas does spiritual warfare operate in your life?
- What personal sins have added to your guilt and frustration?
- How have you dealt with shame?
- What do you use to cover up?
- How do you understand life in the flesh? How does it work for you?
- Invite Jesus into your diagnosis. Ask Him to pull your masks off.

Come Home to the Father

Jesus is asked, "Show us the Father and that will be enough for us" (John 14:8). He answers, "Anyone who has seen me has seen the Father" (v. 9). What does Jesus mean when He calls God "Father"? How does this relate to filling our hole in the soul?

Jesus' revelation of God as Father is unique. It determines His self-consciousness and ministry. Unlike the Old Testament writers who simply saw God as king and judge, Jesus calls Him *Abba*. This Hebrew family word translates as "Pappa" or "Daddy." J. B. Phillips rendered it, "Father, dear Father."[1] By calling God, "Father," Jesus unveils a special relationship that He has with the one, holy God. He is the eternal Son, living in unity and intimacy with God the Father. This is why Jesus says, "All things have been committed to me by my Father. No one knows the Son except the Father, and no one knows the Father except the Son and those to whom the Son chooses to reveal him" (Matt. 11:27).

Jesus continues to bring God as Abba to us today. He offers us the same parent-child relationship that He Himself enjoys. He adopts us into His heavenly family after we are reborn from above. Only this will heal our "being wound"—our shame. This alone will fill the hole in the soul.

Since we are His family members, Jesus teaches us to pray as He prayed, "Our Father in heaven" (Matt. 6:9). Following Jesus, Paul tells the Galatians that God sends the Spirit of His Son into our hearts, crying, "Abba, Father" (4:6). We echo this back:

> For you did not receive a spirit that makes you a slave again to fear, but you received the Spirit of sonship. And by him we cry, "Abba, Father" (Rom. 8:15).

This is the cry of people set free.

Jesus shows us our relationship with the Father in the parable of the prodigal son (see Luke 15:11-32). This story is told to religious leaders who are incensed because of the people Jesus hangs out with. He eats with tax gatherers and sinners. This is His sign of welcome. Rather than condemning these reprobates, He invites them to His table, saying, in effect, "We belong together." This drives religious people crazy. What kind of a God suspends His holy laws to welcome such trash into His presence?

Jesus responds by telling the story of the prodigal. His parable is a confrontational narrative that shows religious people that God loves unconditionally. He is the Father who overcomes our separation from Him by releasing us from our shame and bringing us home to His heart.

It is helpful to look at this dramatic story as if it were a play in three acts. Act 1 shows us the younger son's departure from his father's house. Act 2 shows us his return and reunion with his father. Act 3 shows us his older brother's "religious" reaction and draws the appropriate conclusion. Before the curtain opens on act 1, let's review the biblical text of the story's opening:

> There was a man who had two sons. The younger one said to his father, "Father, give me my share of the estate." So he divided his property between them.
>
> Not long after that, the younger son got together all he had, set off for a distant country and there squandered his wealth in wild living. After he had spent everything, there was a severe famine in that whole country, and he began to be in need. So he went and hired himself out to a citizen of that country, who sent him to his fields to feed pigs. He longed to fill his stomach with the pods that the pigs were eating, but no one gave him anything.
>
> When he came to his senses, he said, "How many of my father's hired men have food to spare, and here I am starving to death! I will set out and go back to my father and say to him: Father, I have sinned against heaven and against you. I am no longer worthy to be called your son; make me like one of your hired men." So he got up and went to his father (vv. 11-20).

ACT 1

As the curtain rises, we see a father with his two sons in the living room of the family home. The younger one says, "Dad, I can't wait for you to die. Give me my share of the estate, and I'm out of here." In other words, he wants out of the relationship to the point of holding a death wish against his dad. It's amazing that this son has the gall to say this to his father. I can't imagine going to my dad with such a request. How would we react if our kids came to us and said, "I want you out of my life. I don't care if you live or die; I want my inheritance now!"? This is exactly what we have done to God by rebelling against Him and going our own way.

Even more surprising, the father actually grants his son's request. This is incomprehensible, but it is exactly what God has done for us. He lets us go, bankrolling us with His providence and provision while we shake our fist and leave.

The younger son lives in the illusion that he'll find freedom far from his father's house. Well-heeled and with a new false self in place, he thinks, *I am my own person. I am independent. I can now self-actualize myself.* Loaded with cash, he departs for a far country.[2] As Helmut Thielicke said, "His deception is in his denial that all that he has comes from his father's hand."[3]

Once in the far country, as long as the younger son has money, he has friends. Unwisely, he exhausts his resources in wild living. Circumstances turn against him. A severe famine sets in. Stripped of everything, he's in dire straits. Finally, in desperation, he finds a job feeding pigs—not a great occupation for a young Jewish boy. (Jewish people considered both pigs and Gentiles, who owned pigs, to be unclean.) As payment, he can eat at the trough with the herd.

I imagine the boy at the trough elbowing the porkers out of the way and thinking, *Things could be better.* In disgrace and despair, he finally comes to himself. At last, circumstances force him to face reality. His life is out of control. He hits bottom. God's intervention begins by breaking through his denial. His illusion of independence is now exposed, and he gets homesick. He remembers how good it really was back at his father's house. Through the crisis, he decides to return home. His rebellion over, he repents.

But the younger son's plans are determined by his view of his father. He believes he can't be restored; after all, he has spent his inheritance and dishonored the family name. Dad's honor must be defended. Justice must be done. Resourceful as ever, he has an idea. Since his father's servants have more than he does, he will go home and say, "Father, I have sinned against heaven and against you. I am no longer worthy to be called your son." His admission of guilt will then lead him to his proposition: "Make me like one of your hired men." While the younger son knows that he will never be restored to the family, he hopes that there will be a hint of compassion in his father's heart. If so, at least he can live with the hired help and have a roof over his head and food on the table.

Notice that through this plan, the son still maintains control. He doesn't simply cast himself on his father's mercy; he goes home to strike a bargain. This bargaining is his subtle sin. Like any codependent, he manipulates, regardless of how self-effacing he appears. Now he starts his return journey as the curtain drops on act 1.

Let's turn back to the biblical text before act 2 begins:

But while he was still a long way off, his father saw him and was filled with compassion for him; he ran to his son, threw his arms around him and kissed him.

The son said to him, "Father, I have sinned against heaven and against you. I am no longer worthy to be called your son."

But the father said to his servants, "Quick! Bring the best robe and put it on him. Put a ring on his finger and sandals on his feet. Bring the fattened calf and kill it. Let's have a feast and celebrate. For this son of mine was dead and is alive again; he was lost and is found." So they began to celebrate (vv. 20-24).

ACT 2

When the curtain rises, the scene shifts back to the father's house. There we see the prodigal's dad faithfully scanning the horizon, hoping to catch a glimpse of his son. As the boy approaches, I imagine that he is nervously rehearsing his little speech written on the cuff of his sleeve: "Father, I have sinned against heaven and against you. I am no longer worthy to be called your son; make me like one of your hired men." Head bowed, he comes up the walk.

The father now does the unthinkable. Spotting his son, he rushes out, throws his arms around him, hugs him and begins to kiss him. The situation appears ludicrous. While the father's body language communicates total love and acceptance, the boy doesn't pick up on this. His view of his father doesn't allow for this kind of a reaction. He is on another track. In his mind, his dad would never act this way. He assumes that he can't be welcomed home and restored to the family. This is faulty thinking, because he doesn't really know his father. He can think of him only as being just and righteous. Similarly, religious people can think of God only as an accountant who keeps an exact ledger of credits and debits. What matters to this holy bookkeeper is performance. They think God approves or disapproves of them based on what they do or don't do, rather than loving them unconditionally for who they are.

While the father bathes his boy in love, the son, unable to compute the hugs and kisses, begins his speech: "Father, I have sinned against heaven and against you. I am no longer worthy to be called your son." No sooner does he admit his guilt than the father cuts him off. All the father wants to hear is, "Dad, I've blown it." The son can't initiate his deal. The picture he had of his father is contradicted as his dad graciously intercepts him.

After his embrace, the father gives his son a signet ring and calls for the servants to get him a new suit of clothes. These gestures restore the younger son's status and identity in the family. Next, the servants kill a fattened calf for a welcome-home party. Later that evening, the younger son walks through the living room, surrounded by his celebrating friends, wondering, *Is this really happening to me? I'm home free and there's a party for me.* The curtain drops on act 2.

Let's read the end of the story from the biblical text before we move on to act 3:

> Meanwhile, the older son was in the field. When he came near the house, he heard music and dancing. So he called one of the servants and asked him what was going on. "Your brother has come," he replied, "and your father has killed the fattened calf because he has him back safe and sound."
>
> The older brother became angry and refused to go in. So his father went out and pleaded with him. But he answered his father, "Look! All these years I've been slaving for you and never disobeyed your orders. Yet you never gave me even a young goat so I could celebrate with my friends. But when this son of yours who has squandered your property with prostitutes comes home, you kill the fattened calf for him!"
>
> "My son," the father said, "you are always with me, and everything I have is yours. But we had to celebrate and be glad, because this brother of yours was dead and is alive again; he was lost and is found" (vv. 25-32).

ACT 3

As the curtain rises on the final act, the older brother has been working on the back 40 all day. He returns home, sees lights and hears music and dancing. A servant reports that his younger brother has come home and been fully restored to the family. Incensed at the news, he defiantly remains outside. Feeling self-justified, like many religious people, he believes in performance for acceptance. He is like a faithful church leader. He ushers every Sunday; he sings in the choir or worship team; he teaches Sunday School; he carries a well-marked Bible; he tithes; he shows up at every meeting; and he reads religious books (even ones on addiction). He is Mr. Faithful—totally predictable. In other words, he's under the Law. When he hears that his renegade younger brother has been welcomed back into the family, he rages at such grace. We can see our codependent, workaholic selves in the older son. We're addicted to performance, hoping to gain God's approval. Fearful that we will never get it, we become hurt and angry.

Back on stage, the father comes out of the house a second time and begs his older son to join the party. Resentful, manipulative, never fulfilled, never satisfied, and filled with "righteous indignation," the older son refuses. Despite all the older son has done, his father has never killed a goat so that he could party with his friends. Is this justice? Where is his reward for his faithfulness? He fumes, *How could my father welcome my blow-it younger brother home? After all, he rebelled against Dad and spent all of his money on prostitutes.* (The mention of prostitutes is new information. Does he know this or, like many of us, is he making assumptions?) Filled with self-justification, the older son parades the history of his faithfulness before his father: He is the model son; he has never rebelled; he is up at the crack of dawn; he always punches in and punches out on time; he has calluses on his hands from working. In short, he has always tried to please his father, hoping to earn his approval. The more he tries to fill the hole in his soul by performing, the larger it becomes.

Like the older brother, we may try to fill our souls with religious performance, but religion never satisfies. It wears us down and wears us out, leaving us exhausted.

As the play ends, the father tells his older son that everything he has is his. All the grace the father extended to the rebellious son is for the self-righteous son as well. It is only proper to welcome back the wayward son with celebration; after all, his return has created an opportunity for grace to pour out from his father's heart. There doesn't need to be any more justification for joy than grace, simply grace. A son has been lost and is now found. He had been dead and is now alive. The younger son is a living example of being loved for who we are rather than for what we do.

The younger son masked his rebellion and fear by leaving home and, in the process, created an independent false self. He thought that when he returned, he would spend his life with the servants. He would be in a kind of purgatory—around the house but never a part of the household. He never imagined that he would be restored to his position in the family—with a party to boot!

His older brother agreed entirely with his view of the father. He remained home, masking his anger and fear of rejection by building his performing false self. He was offended that his father would welcome his blow-it younger brother back home. His father's behavior seemed unjust and irrational. Ironically, this drama reveals that neither son knew his father. Both thought he was a legalistic bookkeeper demanding performance for acceptance. Both confused approval with love. Both were prodigal. The father had to break through both sons' illusions of independence and self-justification, shattering their perceptions of him and of themselves.

The father came out of the house twice. Through this simple gesture, he loved each son equally. He had grace not only for the lost son but also for the "perfect" son. The real difference, then, between the brothers was how each one accepted grace once it had been offered. The younger son was ready and overwhelmed by mercy beyond belief. Since he had nothing more to lose, he had everything to gain by accepting his father's love. The older son, however, resisted his father and refused to join the party. In order to defend his own merit and self-righteousness, he had to retain his picture of what he thought his father should be. Like so many of us today, he was always addictively around the house, but he never joined the party.

> *There is a party waiting for us in our heavenly Father's heart. All we have to do is to go to Him.*

Jesus tells this dramatic story to reveal the heart of God as that of a loving Father. God comes to us in love and wants us to enjoy the party of His free and full grace. Coming home is not a time for fasting; it is a time to sit at His banquet table. The issue is not performance or approval. The issue is massive, boundless, endless love. This is the Father's heart. It's this love that overcomes the abandonment that we all inherit from the Garden of Eden—a reality reinforced by our going our separate ways. But God's love comes with hugs and kisses, which destroy the deep shame produced by our separation from Him. His love releases us from our addictive attachments and welcomes us home. This is the good news that Jesus continues to bring to our craving and codependent selves: There is a party waiting for us in our heavenly Father's heart. He is filled with joy before the holy angels when one sinner repents. All we have to do is to go to Him.

IS IT TRUE?

Is this story about the father and his two sons true? Helmut
Thielicke says that we can believe that it is true because of the
third Son—the Son who tells the story.[4] It is Jesus who comes to
us from the Father's heart. It is Jesus who initiates reconcilia-
tion, running to us, hugging us, kissing us and restoring us to
the family. And where does He do this? He does it at the cross.

The Cross hooked my heart years ago. As a sophomore in
high school, I attended a weekend snow camp sponsored by
Young Life. On Saturday night, Jim Rayburn, Young Life's
founder, narrated in graphic detail how Jesus went through the
absurdity of His trial and extreme physical torture and punishment, and finally how He was stretched naked and nailed up on
a Roman cross, left to die in shame and agony.

Jim went on to say that there were two groups of people at
the cross as Jesus hung there. There was the crowd. They mocked
Him and spit on Him, yelling, "Crucify Him, crucify Him." They
taunted, "Prove Yourself now, Jesus. Come down from that
cross," thinking He could never do it. In effect, they said, "Jesus,
stay on that cross and stay out of our lives."

But there was another group there as Jesus died. It was small:
His mother, Mary, His disciple John and a few women. One criminal, crucified beside Him, cried out, "Jesus, remember me when
you come into your kingdom" (Luke 23:42). This group had not
come to mock. They had come to pray, "Lord, remember me."

Jim said that night that we were all in one group or the other.
We were either in the group saying, "Jesus, stay on the cross and
stay out of my life," or we were in the group praying, "Lord,
remember me." There was no fence to sit on, because there was
no fence.

Now, I knew that I had never gone to the Cross to kneel and
pray. By definition, then, I was in the other group. When I saw

Jesus' love and His sacrifice for my sins, I didn't want to be in that group any longer. I prayed a simple prayer, "Lord, remember me." And He did and does. I came home to the Father's house that night when Jesus came into my heart.

Anyone who has seen me has seen the Father (John 14:9).

Whoever accepts me accepts the one who sent me (13:20).

WELCOME HOME

Most of us have "father issues." Our father may have divorced our mother. He may have been absent or died. He may have been emotionally distant or abusive. I prayed with a young worship leader in London last year. His father pastors a large church. When I asked what I could pray for, he replied in pain, "My father has never told me that he loves me." Perhaps you have never heard that. Or you may have had mixed messages—confusing love and approval.

Jesus has come to bring the Father's heart to you, and it is filled with love. Jesus welcomes you into His own relationship with the Father. He knows the Father who is always present, always loving, always providing, always guiding, always home—and He takes you to the Father, healing the hole in the soul, restoring what was lost through sin and judgment. In Jesus, mercy triumphs. A huge part of our freedom from addiction is to know, experience and rest in the Father's love. Our abandonment is over. This is the healing of our deepest loss and our deepest wound. As Jesus brings the Father to us, we also will begin to recover from any father issues that we carry. God wants to father you, hug you, embrace you and hold you in His Son. Will you let Him do this? Consider the following:

- What has been my relationship with my earthly father?
- What is my relationship with my heavenly Father?
- In what areas of my life do I struggle with grace?
- In what areas of my life have I received grace?
- With whom in Jesus' parable do I identify?
- In what ways does conditional love operate in my relationships?
- How does this hold me back from God's unconditional love?
- Have I gone to the Cross to kneel and pray?
- Do I need to do this right now?
- Do I feel at home with God?
- Have I had a party with Him?

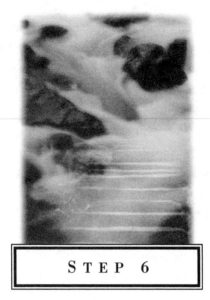

Welcome Your Healing

When we go home to the Father, we meet Him where He meets us—in His Son. And where do we meet the Son? As we have seen, at the Cross. There He dies *for* me, and there I die *to* me. Jesus exchanges His death for my death. Receiving full forgiveness, I die to the flesh: my idols, false self, self-will and shame. I ask Jesus to quiet my cravings, reorder my brain and settle me in His peace. I ask Him to deliver me from the powers of darkness and to help me walk in His light.

Jesus gives me His own position as righteous before the Father. "Not guilty" is stamped on my account. It is paid in full by His blood. As Luther says, "Becoming a Christian is like a wedding."[1] When I am married to Christ by faith, I give Him all I have, and He gives me all He has. I give Him all my sin, and He gives me all His righteousness. Listen to Paul:

> God made him who had no sin [Jesus] to be sin for us, so that in him we might become the righteousness of God (2 Cor. 5:21).

As Jesus' death is mine, so His resurrection is mine. Raised from the dead on the first Easter, He will one day raise me from the dead in the whole new creation. Meanwhile, the reigning Lord reconnects me to God, living in me by His Spirit.

Now in the *position* of righteous, I am in the *process* of becoming righteous (see Rom. 1:17; 8:4). In the words of Dietrich Bonhoeffer, "A Christian is a person who departs from sin and from whom sin departs."[2] This can only happen as Jesus overcomes the power of addiction in my life. It is Jesus who heals the abuse I've experienced. It is Jesus who fills the hole in the soul. How does this happen?

LET THE HEALING BEGIN

First, God breaks through denial. As He intervenes in our lives, reality strikes. We know "we are all addicts in every sense of the

Jesus' cure is deeper than our sickness. He is total help for total need.

word."[3] Second, we repent and detach ourselves from the objects of our addictions. Third, we go through the pain of withdrawal. This means that we experience the opposite of what our addictions give us. If coffee is an upper, to withdraw will be a downer. Without caffeine we will feel depressed until our brain chemistry rebalances. Fourth, we acknowledge any anger or grief over the loss of our addictions. As a psychologist told a friend of mine, "You have to sit in your pain." This means no self-medication. We walk through the loss (with Jesus). Fifth, we ask Jesus to fill the hole in the soul with His Spirit. As we die to our false selves, the fear and shame behind them are exposed, and we are loved to the core. Our abandonment is over. Jesus' cure is deeper than our sickness. He is total help for total need.

LET THE HEALING CONTINUE

Mark 2 records Jesus' healing in four dimensions: forgiveness, family, fun and freedom.

Forgiveness

First, Jesus forgives us and then releases us to forgive others. Before He came, the Jews approached God through the Temple's elaborate blood-sacrifice ritual. Forgiveness was offered to those bringing proper sacrifices for their sins. With Jesus a radical change takes place. Forgiveness is no longer through *ritual* but through *relationship*. It is found in the *person* of Jesus as the Son of God and the *work* of Jesus as the Lamb of God.

Mark tells us that four friends bring a paralyzed man to Jesus and drop him at His feet. Jesus responds, "Son, your sins are forgiven" (Mark 2:5, *NASB*). The religious leaders rightly murmur, "Why does this man speak that way? He is blaspheming; who can forgive sins but God alone?" (v. 7, *NASB*). Exactly. Either Jesus has divine authority to forgive sins, or He is from the devil.

As Jesus pronounces forgiveness, He changes everything. He eliminates the Temple, the sacrificial system and the priesthood by fulfilling them in Himself. But this is not simply a theological shift.

Jesus then commands the man, "Take up your bed and walk" (v. 9, *NKJV*). As he does so, to everyone's amazement, he reveals that forgiveness is our deepest healing. It triggers the rest of the healing that God does in us. Through His sacrificial death, Jesus bridges the gap between God's holiness and our sin. In the words of my friend Jerry Moser, "God zips us open and jumps inside."

The next step in our healing is to not only receive forgiveness but also to give it in return. Jesus teaches us to pray, "Forgive us our debts [sins, trespasses], as we also have forgiven our debtors" (Matt. 6:12). Since He lavishes God's forgiveness on us, for which He paid the highest price, how can we withhold our forgiveness from each other?

Jesus makes this clear when He tells a story about a servant whose master forgives him a debt of millions of dollars. The servant then turns right around and refuses to forgive a man who owes him a few dollars. His hard heart exposed, he is punished without mercy (see Matt. 18:23-34). Like the unforgiving servant, our refusal to forgive means that we never really experienced forgiveness in the first place. (Rather, we probably thought we deserved it.) Pride still grips our lives.

By experiencing Jesus' forgiveness, we then can forgive others. Some years ago, I confronted a church elder about a moral issue in his life. As our conversation ended, he issued a vague threat and then had me fired. Upon my departure from the church, the congregation was dumbstruck, and I was heartbroken. For several weeks I prayed daily, "Lord, help me forgive him." I prayed out of obedience, with little emotion. I prayed so that I could be free from the prison of my unforgiveness.

One evening I rounded a display case at a local video store and there he was. Recovering quickly from surprise, I walked up, greeted him, gave him a hug and went to the parking lot, giddy with joy. My prayers had been answered: Jesus had set my heart free from bitterness and revenge. I moved on.

Family

Second, Jesus heals us by placing us in a whole new family. Religious people see their family as exclusive, needing protection: Since God is holy, we are to be holy like Him. We have to separate ourselves from "sinners." The Jews expressed their holiness by excluding the unclean. After all, a man is known by the company he keeps. Through religious and moral purity, they witnessed to God's laws. This was their special calling in life. Their whole understanding of community was *exclusive*.

Yet Jesus sees God's community as *inclusive*. His relationships aren't based on fear. He doesn't worry about being contaminated or exposed. He is happy to be seen with the "wrong people" and risk His reputation. He eats with our equivalent of loan sharks, drug pushers, illegal aliens, transvestites, prostitutes, inside traders and even terrorists. Jesus invites them to dinner. He actually enjoys hanging out with them.

Doesn't this make you mad? Doesn't this offend you? It certainly offended the religious leaders of His day. The people Jesus is seen with are the people that we wouldn't want to move into our neighborhood. They are the people we wouldn't want our daughters to date. Mark 2:16 says, "When the scribes of the Pharisees saw that He [Jesus] was eating with the sinners and tax collectors, they said to His disciples, 'Why is He eating and drinking with tax collectors and sinners?'" (*NASB*). The religious reaction against Jesus deepens.

Through Jesus, God's heart is open to all. There is now no "them" and no "us." There is no our kind versus their kind. Here is Jesus' reply to the religious people of His day:

It is not those who are healthy who need a physician, but those who are sick; I did not come to call the righteous, but sinners (v. 17, *NASB*).

This means that all of us addicts and idolaters are now welcome in God's family, and it is there that our healing grows. Why?

Because grace embraces everyone, regardless of class, race or social status. To be loved by brothers and sisters who are different from us shatters our pride, isolation, prejudice and artificial boundaries. To be loved by them is to experience Jesus' unconditional love. It is Jesus who brings us together. It is Jesus who is the center of our worship and our common life.

In much of the Church we are not likely to experience this because we are so segregated. While we preach a gospel of justification by faith, we live a gospel of justification by works. To paraphrase C. S. Lewis, we are nice people rather than new people.[4] While we tell each other that God loves us unconditionally, we live out our hidden agendas of performance for acceptance. We confuse unconditional love with conditional love—and it makes us crazy.

Rich Buhler holds that this confusion is perpetuated in families in which approval is substituted for love.[5] As a result, we spend our lives struggling for approval, when what we need is love. Living out the gospel of justification by works apes the larger culture. We are socialized by, "I love you, but . . ." "I love you, but clean up your room." "I love you, but get good grades." "I love you, but go to college." "I love you, but go into daddy's business." "I love you, but marry a blonde (they have more fun)."

I heard a mother thoughtlessly tell her daughter, "If you do this for me, I will love you for life." The implication: If you don't, I'll withdraw my love. This is conditional love, based on performance. Nothing is more controlling or more frightening. Teachers, coaches, pastors, bosses and countless friends use conditional love to prod us to perform or keep us in line. We wonder, *If I fail, will you still love me? If I don't measure up, will I be rejected? Will my shame be exposed?*

Jesus shows us the Father who never says, "I love you, but . . ."
He also gives us a new family in which we learn to love in the same
way. Here we are accepted. Here we are secure. Here is a herd in
which we are safe. Here we belong for time and eternity. Here forgiveness reigns. Here we are grace based. Here we become functional. Here we are reparented. Here we relearn about ourselves in
nonthreatening, nonabusive ways. Rather than being an exclusive
religious family, Jesus' family is inclusive. There is room for you.
There is room for me. His healing continues in community, and it
spreads beyond us to the world that is dying for this kind of love.

Fun

Third, Jesus heals us with fun. I know this sounds shallow, but it
is true. For the Jews, fasting is a sign of piety, but it's not for Jesus'
men. The religious leaders ask, "Why do John's [the Baptist] disciples and the disciples of the Pharisees fast, but Your disciples do
not fast?" (Mark 2:18, *NASB*). What is Jesus' answer? It's party
time.

Remember, Jesus is a tremendously attractive person to be
with. He enjoys all types of people. He tells engaging stories. He
goes to dinner parties and is the life of the party. He tells the
Pharisees that for now fasting is impossible. Being with Jesus is like
being at a wedding where He is the bridegroom. The occasion
demands good food and drink. Let the music play; it's time for
dancing.

Jesus asks, "How can the guests of the bridegroom fast while
he is with them? They cannot, so long as they have him with
them" (v. 19). This is the time of salvation, victory, freedom and
release. It is a time to enjoy the Messiah's presence. It's party time!
It is no longer the Law but the gospel. It is no longer religion but
relationship. It is no longer Moses but a joyful life with Jesus. The
solemnity of long-faced religious processions is over. It is time to
become like little children in order to enter the Kingdom.

Freedom

Fourth, Jesus heals by delivering us from all that is inhuman. Tradition can make us secure, but it also can stifle us. Jewish tradition has grown up around the Law and has suffocated God's people. To light a fire breaks the Sabbath law against working. To thread a needle breaks the Sabbath law against working. Where is the joy in this? Jesus overturns cultural morality. His disciples break legal tradition. Hungry, they pick heads of grain on the Sabbath. This "work" provokes a religious reaction, and "the Pharisees were saying to him, 'Look, why are they doing what is not lawful on the Sabbath?'" (Mark 2:24, *NASB*). Jesus answers that if the Sabbath is made for us, then why would God want us to go hungry on this special day? Besides, it is Jesus, not the religious legalists, who now has authority over the Sabbath:

> The Sabbath was made for man, not man for the Sabbath. So the Son of Man is Lord even of the Sabbath (vv. 27-28).

This restores it to joyous celebration.

Not only are Jesus' followers disobedient, but also He Himself breaks the Sabbath law. He heals a man's withered hand in the synagogue (see Mark 3:1-5). The Pharisees watch to see if Jesus will really go through with it. Wise counsel would tell Him to wait a few hours. Why provoke them? After all, this man has been crippled for a long time. He can hold on a bit longer, and then everybody will be happy. But no. Jesus isn't interested in wise counsel. He is interested in loving this man and making him whole. It is His mission to overturn a religion that thwarts true healing in exchange for a few more empty, pious hours.

This is the last straw for religion. Not only does Jesus center forgiveness in Himself, explode the boundaries of community and party rather than fast, but He also subverts the whole culture of public life. Heretofore, Israel is to reflect God's actions in her actions. Since He rested on the Sabbath, the Jews are to rest on the Sabbath. But with Jesus, the whole structure collapses. God's actions are clearly reflected now as mercy triumphs over traditional rules. Matters of the heart replace habit. Mourning turns into joy. For religious people to live, Jesus has to die:

> The Pharisees went out and immediately began conspiring with the Herodians against Him, as to how they might destroy him (v. 6, *NASB*).

SO WHAT?

It is common to contrast religion with Jesus. "Religion" is our seeking God. It is life in the flesh. It is life centered on us and our own self-justification. Religion then becomes a vehicle for our addictive selves. We use religious practices, aesthetics and morality to fill the hole in the soul. We use religion to manipulate God and gain position before Him. As we become religious, we say to Him, "Look at my piety, my faith and my obedience. This ought to impress You. (It impresses my friends.) This ought to give me standing with You. You are lucky to have me on Your team."

We try to impress God and each other in order to overcome our shame and the addictions that cover it. But these tricks don't work. We are never delivered from addiction through morality or sheer discipline. As the world struggles with addiction, it asks the questions, *What* will deliver me? Will Alcoholics Anonymous (A.A.) or Narcotics Anonymous (NA) or Al-Anon deliver me? Will the Twelve Steps deliver me? Will a recovery group deliver me? Will therapy deliver me? Will medication deliver me? All of these may offer help at a given moment, but they don't address the bottom line. There is no "what" that will deliver us from addiction. A "what" merely becomes the next object of our attachment as we exchange one addiction for another. When we ask, *What* will deliver me? we ask the wrong question. It's not "what" but "who." Trapped in bondage, unable to do the good, Paul cries out, "Who will deliver me from this body of death?" (Rom. 7:24, *NKJV*). Our deepest need is not for a program but for a person. Only after we answer the question, *Who* will deliver me? are we ready for the healthy support and spiritual disciplines that others can give us.

THE GREAT RESTORATION

Jesus is the "who." He delivers us. He overturns the religion of this addictive, dysfunctional world, bringing the Almighty to us as our loving Father and restoring our relationship with Him. Jesus bridges the gulf created by our abandonment of God and His abandonment of us, and He destroys the resulting shame. His wrath—His "no"—is the next to the last word.[6] The last word is His word of grace—His "yes." Rather than waiting for us to come to Him or to get better, God takes the initiative. He pursues us in Jesus.

We ask the question, But why is this so hard to believe? Many of us are socialized in churches that are not grace based. They insist on our sacramental duties, moral obedience, faithful attendance, evangelical fervor, social responsibility and financial support. As we have seen, this is the lived-out lifestyle of justification by works.

Peggy, a pastor's daughter, came to me for counseling. She was in pain. I asked her what it was like growing up in the Church. She told me that when she was a small girl a woman had caught her drawing in a hymnal. She scolded, "You shouldn't be doing that; you're the pastor's daughter!" Later, when she started school, her friends' response to her was "Watch it! Her father's a pastor!" As expectations piled up, she withdrew. I suspected that

Peggy could hardly believe in God's unconditional love for her. She had little sense of grace.

With this in mind, I proposed the following situation. "Peggy, what if you came home on a Friday night, dead drunk, blasted out of your mind? You opened the door, staggered in and vomited all over the carpet. Now suppose Jesus was there in the flesh. What would He do?"

Peggy was silent for a long moment. Beads of sweat appeared on her forehead. Her muscles tensed and she frowned. Finally, she choked out her answer: "He would be angry!"

After a pause, I asked Peggy if I could tell her what I thought Jesus would do. She agreed. "First," I told her, "He would put you to bed. Then He would clean up the vomit. Finally, when you woke up in the morning, He would put His arms around you and ask, 'Peggy, where does it hurt?'" In a crisis, Jesus is there to hold us and take us to the Father.

Life with Jesus is both crisis and process. He is our perfection, and we strive to become like Him. For addicts, this process includes giving up control daily, detaching from compulsions and accepting God's free, holy love. When will it all end? Only when we are face-to-face with the "who" who delivers us.

BE HEALED!

Since the Christian life is crisis and process, I need to process the meaning of grace. So much of the world and the Church, as we have seen, do not love unconditionally. Unconditional love is radical beyond belief. Only God Himself can speak this into my life. Only God Himself can bear His life-changing witness to its reality. Consider the following:

- How have I been socialized by conditional love?
- Do I have a hard time distinguishing love from approval?

- When have I been manipulated by the control and demands of others, fearing loss or rejection?
- When has grace come to me? How have I recognized it?
- Who is a sign of grace in my life?
- What keeps me fearful, performing?
- Have I received Jesus' radical word of forgiveness?
- Is my community inclusive? How does this show itself?
- Where does legalism rear its ugly head in my life?
- What tempts me to act "religious"? How do I deal with this?
- Am I looking for a "what" to set me free?
- How do I answer Paul's question, "Who will deliver me?"

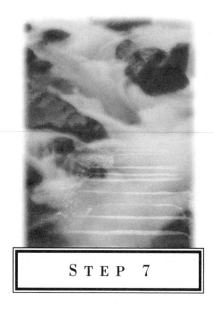

S T E P 7

Live Fearlessly with the Fearless Jesus

Stanton Peele says that addicts are basically fearful.[1] Since "we are all addicts in every sense of the word," we are all fearful.[2] Behind our bravado, our self-confidence and our need to control lurk deep fears.

As we have seen, since the Fall, our sense of security has gone amok. The herd instinct may lead us to huddle together, but, at the same time, fear drives us apart. We are afraid of exposing the shame base of our lives. We hide the hole in the soul; we cover up. We use addictive activities, substances and relationships to calm our nerves and fill our emptiness. This fear of exposure triggers other fears: abandonment, rejection, failure, loss, disease, aging, death and our future beyond the grave.

For those of us whose landscaped brains carry unmet childhood needs and who have been marked by assault and abuse, fear puts us over the top. Intense stress keeps us on red alert. Millions suffer from anxiety disorders, phobias and panic attacks and withdraw into protective shells. This can lead to agoraphobia: the fear of open spaces, crowds, driving and even leaving the house. Life narrows down or shuts down.

As we come to Jesus, since He is fearless, He will help us deal with our fears. We need His confidence and His sense of security in our lives. We need Him to become our sponsor. What does that mean?

If we are an alcoholic in A.A., we are to look for a sponsor. We target a person with years of sobriety who has qualities in his or her life that we would like to have in ours. We see if they will commit to being our sponsor. To sponsor someone is demanding. Do you want to drink? Call your sponsor. Are you lonely? Call your sponsor. Do you have questions? Call your sponsor.

Analogously, we ask Jesus to become our sponsor. He has in His life what we need in ours. He will always be there for us. He will share our loneliness. He will answer our questions. He will invest His love, His wisdom and His power in our lives. Fear begins to leave as we turn to the fearless Jesus. But how does that happen?

COME OUT OF FEAR WITH JESUS

Fear is rooted in the shame base of our lives. As a result, we are subject to stress and anxiety that Jesus will relieve. In Him we are abandoned no more! He breaks through our shame and begins to set us free.

To be sure, not all fears in this fallen world are destructive. To fear walking alone at night, to fear our car's breaking down on a lonely road, to fear a violent stranger or an abusive parent gives us needed protection. Yet many fears are debilitating. How, then, can Jesus help us?

Jesus Restores Our Lost Identity

First, when we make Jesus our sponsor, He restores our lost identity. If we don't have a firm grasp on who we are, where we have come from and where we are going, we are constantly plagued by fear: Am I fitting into the crowd? Am I performing properly at work? Will I make the team? Does this dress look good on me? Does he or she love me? What am I going to do with my life? The questions and doubts go on and on; fear stalks us at every turn.

Jesus, our sponsor, however, is free from these fears. He knows that He is the eternal Son of God, loved by the Father. He knows that He has come from the Father and is going to the Father, and He knows why He is here (see John 13:1-3). He has come to proclaim the message of the Kingdom—God's rule is now within reach—and to minister the Kingdom by casting out demons and healing the sick (see Mark 1:14-15; 3:14). He has come to save that which is lost (see Matt. 18:12). Secure in His identity and destiny, He secures us—at the core of our being—by uniting us to Himself. Here are His promises:

1. We are fully forgiven (see Rom. 8:1).
2. We are adopted into His family (see Rom. 8:15).
3. We participate in His relationship with the Father (see Rom. 8:15-17).

As we receive His message, we share His ministry. We begin to do what Jesus does. Furthermore, we grow in intimacy with Him. Paul says that the Holy Spirit witnesses to our spirits that we are sons and daughters of God (see Rom. 8:16). John wrote, "Behold what manner of love the Father has bestowed on us, that we should be called children of God!" (1 John 3:1, *NKJV*). We belong to Him for time and eternity.

We not only are called to be with Jesus, but we also are called to be like Jesus. He is transforming us on the inside by His Spirit. He is conforming us to Himself. Jesus then brings a deep, lasting security. He drives away the fears of not knowing who we are and where we are going. He shows us how to live in this world.

As we have seen, Jesus expresses His relationship to the Father by calling Him Abba, His intimate family name. He invites us to address God in the same way. Howell Harris described his experience while praying:

> I felt suddenly my heart melting within me, like wax before the fire, with love to God my Savior. I felt not only love and peace, but also a *longing* to be dissolved, and to be with Christ; and there was a cry in my inmost soul, with which I was totally unacquainted before, it was this—Abba, Father; Abba, Father! I could not help calling God *my* Father; I knew that I was his child, and that he loved me; my soul was being filled and satiated. . . . I could now say that I was happy indeed.[3]

As we become secure in the Father's love and become more and more intimate with Him, Jesus also deals with the storms of life that have landscaped our brains. He begins healing the abuse, assault, judgments and losses that have imprinted us, restoring the biochemical balance of our craving brain.

Drew Pinsky says that childhood pain is timeless. He described a patient who suffered from such pain:

> The pain that started with the traumas of . . . childhood was still going on in the present. It still is felt raw and fresh. It happened then, it was happening now, and

as far as his brain was concerned it was going to keep on happening in the future.[4]

Like Pinsky's patient, we also may find ourselves right back in the place of abuse. But since Jesus is the eternal Son, He lives outside of time. He can move back into our past through the power of His Spirit and set us free from our protective fears and the pain they mask.

An Episcopal priest, introverted and gripped by childhood fears, attended a healing seminar led by Francis MacNutt. Skeptical, he listened with significant reserve. Finally, he decided to have Francis pray for him. As Francis prayed, the Holy Spirit took the priest into a deep spiritual place. He saw the schoolyard where he was continually beaten up as a child, and fear flooded him again. As he looked, some bullies came toward him. He looked again and Jesus was standing with him. Then Jesus stepped between him and the bullies and said to them, "If you have to hit somebody, hit Me." With that his fear was broken. He was set free from lifelong pain. At last his identity was secure in Jesus.

Jesus Helps Us Cope with Stress

Second, when we make Jesus our sponsor, He helps us deal with the stress of daily living. Since He is the truth, He speaks the truth and frees us to do the same. He is not afraid of His family, friends or followers. He relates to them out of His deep security that stems from His relationship with His Father. When His mother and brothers try to restrain Him, thinking He is crazy, He responds that His true family consists of those who do the Father's will (see Mark 3:20-35). The home crowd loves His teaching until He tells them that although many are sick in Israel, God's heart is also for outcast Gentiles (see Luke 4:23-30).

Later, although He gives Simon a new name—Peter, the Rock—He also tells Peter that he is Satan's tool when he tries to keep Him from suffering and dying in Jerusalem (see Matt. 16:18,23; Mark 8:33; John 1:42). In all of this, Jesus doesn't avoid confrontation. He hasn't a trace of codependency. He knows that the truth sets us free and releases us from our fears. He also calls us to be truth tellers.

When I was in Wichita, Kansas, I was tempted to avoid the truth. A friend asked me to chat about Jesus with a man named Jeff. As we talked, his objections to the gospel melted. I sensed that he was ready to ask Jesus into his life. But I hesitated because he had a live-in girlfriend. I wondered, *Should I bring her up? What if I lose him at this point?* Jesus didn't let me off the hook. Truth overcame my fears and I said, "Before we pray, I need to ask you about your girlfriend." He replied, "If I trusted someone who loved me and would tell me what to do, I would do it." With this, he asked Jesus into his life. Within a day he moved out of his living situation. Two months later his girlfriend became a Christian, and shortly thereafter they were married. Jesus had called me to accountability. As with the Samaritan woman and her live-in lover, the truth set Jeff free.

As we make Jesus our sponsor, He deals with our fears of people. He confronts our codependent relationships. We give up our people-pleasing attitudes and refuse to live our lives according to others' agendas. We no longer have to guard our family secrets of alcoholism or abuse. We no longer have to gossip in order to draw attention to ourselves. We no longer have to "triangulate," telling people to speak for us out of our fear of rejection.

Jesus not only fearlessly proclaims the truth as He announces the Kingdom, but He also ministers the Kingdom in the Spirit's power. He brings God's rule against satanic darkness. Fearlessly, He drives out demons, heals the sick and restores all that the enemy has stolen. As the devil's counterfeit kingdom is plundered, God's kingdom advances. When we submit to His rule, fear leaves.

With Jesus as our sponsor, we minister the Kingdom by the Spirit's power. We no longer run from people's wounds, sores and pain. We move toward them with love, mercy and healing. As Paul promised Timothy, "For God did not give us a spirit of timidity, but a spirit of power, of love and of self-discipline" (2 Tim. 1:7). We also will lose our fear of demons (as well as, perhaps, our skepticism about them).

This happened to me when I met a medium from the Caribbean who was trained by her grandmother and aunt. She held numerous séances. After her conversion, she was plagued by her past. She tried to burn herself to death. A fellow pastor brought her

We need no longer fear the darkness.

to me for healing prayer. I led her to renounce all of her occult practices. We broke curses and hexes that had been placed on her by her family. Then I asked her to name the spirits that she had communicated with during her séances. One by one I ordered them out in Jesus' name. As the last one left, it literally hurled her across the room, and she crashed into the wall. She was finally free. At this, we were not only shaken but also amazed and grateful. As Jesus empowers us to face the darkness, His truth turns on the lights. His enemies have to flee, and God's rule is extended over Satan's former domain. We need no longer fear the darkness.

When Jesus filled me with His Spirit and called me to share in His kingdom ministry, I had to confront my fears: What happens if I invite people to Christ and nobody comes? What happens if I pray for the sick and nobody gets healed? Over the years I have seen many come to Christ and I have seen many healed. But at other times, I have not seen a single person come to Christ or be healed. My fear of failure no longer holds me back. I know that I am called to obedience—to bring Jesus' message and ministry of the Kingdom. The rest lies in His hands. This releases me to focus on Jesus and the people He wants me to love rather than on myself.

At a dinner party a few years ago, I was engaged in a superficial conversation with one of the elders of my church. Suddenly the thought flashed through my mind to ask him if he were having an affair. He was shocked at my question, but I was even more shocked at his answer. "Yes," he confessed. He went on to say that he had been praying for two weeks for the courage to confess this to someone. I was the answer to that prayer. Our conversation led to repentance, accountability and the restoration of his marriage. In that moment, Jesus overcame my fears and allowed me to share in His healing work.

Jesus is not only fearless with His friends and those seeking help, but He is also fearless with His enemies. He doesn't dodge confrontation. He calls King Herod a "fox" (Luke 13:32). He tells the religious leaders that they "are like whitewashed tombs, which look beautiful on the outside but on the inside are full of dead men's bones and everything unclean" (Matt. 23:27). When He is on trial for His life, He takes command, declares Himself to be the Son of God and seals His fate (see Matt. 26:64; Mark 14:62; Luke 22:67-70). He then endures unspeakable suffering, torture and death, praying from the cross, "Father, forgive them" (Luke 23:34).

As we make Jesus our sponsor, we too can deal with our enemies in His fearless fashion. His command for us to love our enemies and pray for them will not fall on deaf ears. Fears for our own safety and well-being will be overcome as Jesus gives us grace to stand up for Him.

I attended a Nichiren Shoshu Buddhist meeting in Hollywood one night. Crammed into a large living room, several dozen converts and inquirers sang heartily. Then their evangelist delivered an enthusiastic message about the special benefits of chanting. He told us that if we joined him, regardless of our beliefs, we would get what we chanted for because we would be aligned with the natural forces of the universe. He promised, "Chant for a car and you will get a car; chant for a girl and you will get a girl." Then he asked if anyone had a question.

I raised my hand and asked, "If I were dying of cancer and had five minutes to live, what would you have to say to me?" Dodging my question, he replied, "We are interested in life. Chant for a car and you will get a car." I raised my hand again, "I don't feel you answered my question. What do you have to say about death?" He responded, "We talk about life, not death. Anyway, no one has come back from the dead to tell us." "You're wrong," I replied. "One has come back from the dead. Jesus Christ. And He told us." With this, he closed the meeting and ushered me out. I felt both joy and relief as I exited. It was the fearless Jesus who had taken my fears and replaced them with His truth and the power to speak it. Who knows who heard the truth in that room that night?

While Jesus lives in constant communion with the Father and bears the authority of the Kingdom, He exercises that authority in love. His service is neither manipulative nor self-gratifying. He doesn't mask anger by pious good deeds. After John tells us that Jesus knows that He came from God and is going to God, he tells us that Jesus lays aside His garments, takes a towel and basin and washes His disciples' feet. They are shocked and dismayed at His humble service. At first Peter refuses to let Him do it, but Jesus breaks his pride by serving him (see

John 13:1-8). He also models how we are to serve in His name.

Some years ago, my friend Gary was inducted into the army. Before he left we had dinner together, and as the evening ended, he went into the bathroom and came back with a damp towel and a bar of soap. Kneeling before me, he began to untie my shoes. For a moment I was confused. Then I remembered Jesus' final night with His disciples. Embarrassment welled up inside of me. I wanted to say, "Stop. Don't." I thought, *My socks are dirty; my feet smell*. As I sat there and let Gary wash my feet, my shame and protest melted. I then felt a profound love and gratitude for this brother. Through his humble act, I saw Jesus, and He broke my pride that night.

With Jesus as our sponsor, we die daily to our false selves and live more and more fearlessly, sharing His message and mission as we humbly serve others. We are secure in Him and we can trust Him to deal with the daily stress in our lives. Walking in His truth sets us free.

Jesus Balances Out Our Emotions

Third, because Jesus is fearless, He is not only free to say what He thinks and live it out, but He is also free to feel what He feels. He has never been shut down emotionally by abuse. He was never told, as my mother told me, "If you can't say something nice, don't say it at all." He is always His authentic self and helps us to be the same.

The Gospel writers have no special interest in Jesus' emotional life. They offer us no psychological profile. Yet, in passing, they show us a healthy human being who experiences a full range of feelings.

Often the Gospels speak of Jesus' love for people. John tells us, "Jesus loved Martha and her sister and Lazarus" (11:5). When a rich young man comes to Jesus seeking eternal life, Mark says, "Jesus felt a love for him" (10:21, *NASB*). The Gospels also speak of Jesus' "compassion." This word means to feel a deep love in our inward parts, at the center of our emotions. Jesus has this for the crowds "because they were distressed and dispirited like sheep without a shepherd" (Matt. 9:36, *NASB*). He feeds the multitude and raises a widow's son from the dead out of the same compassion (see Mark 6:33-44; Luke 7:11-17).

At the other extreme, Jesus feels anger. He is angry and "deeply distressed" at the religious leaders who judge Him for healing on the Sabbath (3:5). He is angry at the corruption He found in the Temple as He drives out the moneychangers and animals being sold (see Matt. 21:12-13). But Jesus' anger is always moral. It is directed at sin and its consequences.

Jesus also feels great joy. Luke tells us of a time, after Jesus' disciples had cast out demons, when Jesus felt joy: "Jesus, full of joy through the Holy Spirit, said, 'I praise you, Father, Lord of heaven and earth, because you have hidden these things from the wise and learned, and revealed them to little children. Yes, Father, for this was your good pleasure'" (10:21). Through His story of the shepherd who finds his stray sheep, Jesus expresses His own joy at the lost's being found (see 15:7). When the prodigal son comes home, his father throws a party (see vv. 22-24). No wonder Jesus promises His followers, "I have told you this so that my joy may be in you and that your joy may be complete" (John 15:11).

Jesus also feels grief. He weeps at Lazarus' tomb (see John 11:35). He weeps over His vision of Jerusalem in ruins (see Luke 19:41-42). Facing death, His heart is troubled and tormented in the garden of Gethsemane. Luke wrote, "And being in anguish . . . his sweat was like drops of blood falling to the ground" (22:44).

As we make Jesus our sponsor, He will heal our emotions. As He breaks our pride with His serving love, paradoxically, He also opens us up. We can cry and laugh again. The hardness, the self-protection, the false front and the attempts to always be in control begin to go. We become childlike again—spontaneous, free, in touch with Him and with each other. Conversely, if we are on an emotional roller coaster, He will balance us out as we become more and more secure in Him.

In summary, when we make Jesus our sponsor, He deals with us fearlessly. He secures our identity in Himself. He exposes our wounds and the shame that covers them. Then He begins to heal us. He breaks down our walls as He breaks our hearts. He intrudes into our lives and never lets us go. Denial, avoidance and repression no longer work well for us.

Jesus always tells us the truth, and with that, He sets us free. As we welcome what He has in His life into our lives, little by little He turns us into fearless people. The opinions and agendas of family and friends no longer control us. This is a lifelong process. We join Him in confronting the confusion, deception and lies of this world. We are never alone. As Paul said, nothing can separate us from His love (see Rom. 8:39).

GET COMMITTED

Have you made Jesus your sponsor? Are you patterning your life after His? Is He your role model? Do you want His qualities and values in your life? Will you commit yourself to His message and ministry? We all must answer these questions. If we don't follow Jesus, we are left with broken, fragmented, contradictory people to pattern our lives after. In our sickness, we are tempted to be like the sick people around us and think that is healthy. Often we suppose that there are no alternatives. We are stuck with the impact of our dysfunctional families and friends, and the perversions of popular culture.

Sometimes people we admire are unavailable or unapproachable. They are too important, too busy or too popular to spend time with us. But Jesus is just the opposite. He not only wants our commitment, time and affection, but He also gives us His. And He really is the world's only fully functional person. God is absolutely resolved to make us like His Son. As this begins to happen, our fears begin to dissipate.

- Have you asked Jesus to be your sponsor?
- What do you see in Jesus that you would like to see in yourself? Ask Him to make the necessary changes so that you look like Him.
- In what areas of life do you experience fear?
- What would it mean for you to be fearless about what you think and feel?
- How much of your life is run by other people's opinions about you?
- Are you a people pleaser? How has this worked for you?
- What would it be like to live without ungodly fear?
- Ask God to rewire your brain and free you from any excessive anxiety and stress.
- Ask God to make you more like Jesus.

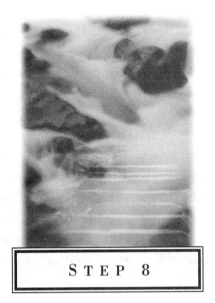

Live Free with the Free Jesus

Billy had bloodshot eyes, a bloated face, scraggly hair and open sores. He lived in an alley near my office. His rage made him passive aggressive, but he had a tender heart. He was an alcoholic and very sick. He had contracted AIDS. Seizures often landed him in the hospital until an infection finally killed him. A pump house at the beach displayed his spray-painted memorial. To his friends he had been a cosmic king, free from family (very abusive), work, responsibility and any commitment beyond himself. But had he really been free?

Humanists assume that freedom means the liberty to do whatever we please (as long as no one gets hurt—but "hurt" remains undefined). If our reason is clear and our will is free, our only limitations are physical. Karl Marx, however, believed that we are determined by economic forces, and Sigmund Freud held that we are the prisoners of our unconscious drives. For Freud, freedom is simply our adjustment to life's pain.

From our study of addiction, however, and our reading of the Bible, it is clear that we are all in bondage. Since the Fall, there is no "natural" freedom. Only by God's gracious intervention can we detach ourselves from the things and people that control us. Rather than suffering from the bondage of desire, we experience the freedom of desire. This means that we will not turn any process, substance or relationship into an idol. We give

Real freedom isn't found in independence or separation from God but in communion with Him.

up all forms of control to the control of God. Freedom means that we are able to think, say and feel truthfully without fear of abandonment or shame. Deep within, we know that Jesus loves us unconditionally and that we are secure in Him.

Now we can at last love God with all our hearts, souls and minds, and love our neighbors as ourselves.

How can we nurture this freedom? How can we prevent relapse into addiction and codependency? First, we must make Jesus our sponsor and live with Him—the only fully free person—day by day. In His freedom, we will be set free from our cravings, attachments, compulsions and addictions.

Jesus' freedom is paradoxical. He is absolutely submitted to His Father. Since this submission is born out of love, He is absolutely free in it. Jesus' love for the Father comes from the Father. It is self-giving love. He prays, "You loved me before the creation of the world" (John 17:24). In response to this love, He speaks what the Father speaks and does what the Father does. In fact, all He does comes as a gift from the Father's heart. Jesus' freedom is in open communion with His Father, and it serves as the Father's channel for what He wants accomplished. This fulfills His destiny. This is His freedom.

Jesus' freedom is grounded in His identity with the Father. He is never in doubt about the Father's love for Him. The Father never withholds love from Jesus for His own good. Jesus never teaches or heals with one eye on the Father, hoping to see Him cheering from the grandstands. Jesus is free also from any external code. He has no need to gauge how people feel about Him in order to know how He feels about Himself. He is free from the need to win approval both from the Father and from people.

Unlike addictive, codependent people, Jesus has no illusion of control. Submitted to the Father, He doesn't have to get control of Himself. This frees Him from seeking to control circumstances or people. Fear of failure, exposure or losing His addictive fix isn't a hook for Him. Certain of who He is, Jesus is free from our control and expectations. He is free to love, confront, comfort, heal and save us.

Through Jesus' example, as He becomes our sponsor, we learn that freedom isn't found in independence or separation from God. Real freedom is found in communion with God. No wonder Jesus says that apart from Him we can do nothing (see John 15:5). God made us for relationship and rulership. To exercise this under His sovereignty is to be the free people we were created to be. To understand Jesus' freedom and to live it out by

His Spirit, we need to look at the negative side and then the positive side of His freedom.

WHAT JESUS IS FREE FROM

The Devil

To begin with, Jesus is free from bondage to the devil. He exposes Satan as a murderer. All death wishes, suicidal compulsions and violence toward creation reflect Satan's hostility to God's order of life and offer of eternal life through His Son. Jesus also exposes Satan as a liar and the father of lies (see John 8:44). He is the source of all deception. Into this death and darkness, Jesus speaks the truth that liberates us today.

Free from Satan's control, Jesus ransacks his kingdom. He breaks the control of afflicting spirits and orders them out. Often these power encounters involve incredible force. People go into convulsions as the shrieking devils leave. Physical and emotional healing are the result. Jesus straightens a woman bent over by a spirit for 18 years (see Luke 13:11-13). He finds a man hosting an army of demons and leaves him clothed and in his right mind (see Mark 5:15).

With Jesus as our sponsor, we will be increasingly free from Satan. We will become wise to his schemes. We will discern the presence of evil spirits. Demons hooked to our spirits will have to leave. Whether they leave at conversion or some time later through repentance and renunciation, we can pull up the welcome mat and order them out in Jesus' name.

Tim was afflicted by demons through childhood abuse and years of drug addiction. He was now dying from his addiction. A psychologist friend, Dr. Joe Ozawa, asked me if we had ever prayed for Jim's deliverance. My answer was no. But since we had tried everything else, I agreed to ask Tim if he would be open to this kind of prayer. When I approached him, he reported that in a recent dream he had seen several demons leave his body. Now he was ready for us. The following week, Joe and I prayed for him and eight spirits left him. The next morning I called him up and he said, "Don, for the first time in years, I have no desire to do cocaine." Today, Tim is a professional drug counselor.

Sadly, Christians may relapse into satanic bondage and need deliverance prayer again. Paul exhorted the Ephesians to "not give the devil an opportunity" or handle on their lives (4:27, *NASB*). Although we war against spiritual forces, we must not live in paranoia. If we resist the devil, he will flee from us. Jesus will set us free and keep us free.

The World

Jesus also is free from bondage to this fallen world. As the King bearing the Kingdom, He challenges all other earthly kingdoms. This includes the often-idolatrous kingdom of the family, parental approval and control. While Jesus' parents sense His unique destiny, He nevertheless breaks from them early in life. At 12 years of age, He vanishes from their traveling party. Returning to the Temple in Jerusalem, He debates the scholars. Since Jesus is free from codependency, when Mary and Joseph find Him, He replies to their concerns explaining that He has to be about His heavenly Father's business (see Luke 2:41-49). No wonder Jesus says, "Whoever does God's will is my brother and sister and mother" (Mark 3:35). Again, He warns, "If anyone comes to me and does not hate his father and mother, his wife and children, his brothers and sisters—yes, even his own life—he cannot be my disciple" (Luke 14:26).

As our sponsor, Jesus demands that we break from idolatrous family controls and find new life in Him. He creates our moral and spiritual boundaries. Our families may become enemies when they can no longer control us. Again, Jesus warns, "Brother will betray brother to death, and a father his child; children will rebel against their parents and have them put to death. All men will hate you because of me" (Matt. 10:21-22).

This violence comes from the shame that has been transmitted to us by our parents. They have used it to bind us with their judgments. The controls of conditional love and withheld approval have enforced their demands. This has left us emotionally and spiritually broken. Coming to Christ may ostracize us from our natural families. I know a young woman who was threatened with disinheritance if she continued in her faith. This pressure led her to live far from home. It also was a source of her own spiritual maturity.

Legalism

Jesus is also free from the kingdom of religious legalism, with its bitter fruit of either pride ("look how religious I am") or guilt ("look how I've failed again"). Legalism traps us in perfectionism and performance. Caught in these responses, we live outside ourselves, fearful of what others may think. We hide behind the false self of religious piety, seeking our own self-justification. Addicted to institutional approval and control, our guilt is only relieved by our performance, and it is never enough. Jesus warns us about the clergy who don't do what they say they'll do. He also warns us about the Pharisees who look good but are addicted to their own self-image. Only grace can free us from such performance. As our sponsor, Jesus models this for us and gives it to us as we walk with Him.

Money

Jesus is also free from the kingdom of money. He is free from the fear of losing things and the fear of scarcity. As a celibate, itinerant prophet, His needs are simple. He knows that His heavenly Father will take care of Him. Having no permanent home, He relies on the graciousness of others. Consistent with

His own poverty, He warns that idolatry and oppression of riches make it hard for a wealthy man to enter the kingdom of God (see Matt. 19:24; Mark 10:23-25; Luke 18:24-25). Even while most of His followers raise families, own property and live settled lives, they, like Jesus, can't serve both God and money. It is not only Jesus' intention to bring down the idol of materialism for His generation but also to deliver us from a similar bondage to money today. He promises that our heavenly Father will clothe us like the lilies of the field and watch over us like a hawk. If we seek God's kingdom and righteousness first, all else will follow (see Matt. 6:28-33; Luke 12:27-31). Like His disciples, most of us will marry and have money, and if we don't allow this money to control us, we will enjoy the same provision the Father lavished on Jesus.

Money and material security have been a real idol in my life. I am a Depression baby. My parents saw people lose everything in the crash of 1929. As a result, I was always afraid of scarcity and was conservative in my spending habits. When God clearly called me to leave a former church, I only had a small income from part-time college teaching. There was no way Kathryn and I could live on my income. Having the deep assurance that the Lord had released me, after resigning, I walked to my office. There I found a note to call my lawyer friend Randy in Houston, Texas. As we talked, he asked me about my situation. Without sharing any financial need, I told him that my wife and I were on a new adventure with the Lord. He responded, "Come up with a budget. See what more you need. Ann and I will make up the difference." They did so for several years. Every check reminded me of Jesus' promise—He will provide and always has.

False Values

Jesus is also free from the kingdom of this fallen world with its false values of power, pride and control. He is free from its demands of performance for acceptance, and as our sponsor, He can set us free as well. Transparency and truth are His weapons. They expose the lies of our lives. For Jesus, every idol must go. Every unhealthy attachment must be broken. He is relentless. He wants it all and will have it all. This fallen world has no claim on Him, and it is to have no claim on us. He is Lord.

Sin

Jesus is also free from the bondage of sin. He is the sinless Son of God. While He is a man of utter humility, He never is conscious of sin. He never asks for forgiveness as He forgives others their sins. In this, as C. S. Lewis shows, Christ assumes that all evil is ultimately committed against Him, a position that only God can hold.[1] If someone came to me and said, "Don, I've stolen money from my company," and I replied, "I forgive you," this would be absurd. The sin wouldn't be against me. It would be against the company and against the law, but most important, it would be against God who says, "Thou shalt not steal" (Exod. 20:15, *KJV*). As Jesus shows us, all sin is against Him, and He alone can forgive it.

Jesus' sinlessness means that He continually does the will of the Father. Out of this perfect communion, He says, "Don't you believe that I am in the Father, and that the Father is in me? The words I say to you are not just my own. Rather, it is the Father, living in me, who is doing his work" (John 14:10). Jesus prays before the cross, "I have brought you glory on earth by completing the work you gave me to do" (17:4). Peter adds, "Christ suffered for you. . . . 'He committed no sin, and no deceit was found in his mouth'" (1 Pet. 2:21-22).

The heart of the gospel is that the sinless Jesus takes our sins upon Himself and in return gives us forgiveness and freedom. We gain ownership of this forgiveness and freedom when we humble ourselves, repent and confess our sins. With clean hearts, freedom from guilt is ours.

Since Jesus is sinless, He is free from the bondage of the Law. He keeps it effortlessly: "Do not think that I have come to abolish the Law or the Prophets; I have not come to abolish them but to fulfill them" (Matt. 5:17). Living in perfect communion with the Father, His obedience isn't religious. It comes spontaneously from His heart. He concludes, "Be perfect, therefore, as your heavenly Father is perfect" (v. 48). Standing alone, we will be driven to despair. How can we burn with the same moral purity as God? But we need to move from despair to admitting that we have no power over our lives. This drives us to Jesus. He is the perfect One, and we only can be perfect in Him. Our obedience to the Law now comes through Him—from His gift of grace.

Dietrich Bonhoeffer teaches that before we come to Christ, we have a *direct* relationship to the Law.[2] Its demands are laid on us, and we struggle with obedience and carry the guilt of disobedience. When we come to Christ, we have an *indirect* relationship with the Law. Jesus stands between us and the demand of God.[3] He is our mediator. He adds only one thing: He keeps the Law and fulfills it in Himself. Now we can begin to keep it through Him and the power of His Spirit. This happens, as Paul says, because Christ sacrificed Himself for our sins and lifts our condemnation, "in order that the righteous requirements of the law might be fully met in us, who do not live according to the sinful nature but according to the Spirit" (Rom. 8:4).

The Flesh

Finally, Jesus is free from the bondage to the flesh, the craving instincts and the false front that covers our shame-based lives. He lives without addictive attachments and corrupt desires. He lives in complete dependence on the Father. Secure in His identity and destiny, He gives Himself away. Rather than meeting His own needs—as we are manipulated to do by our consumer culture—He comes to do the Father's will by freely meeting the needs of others.

Empowered by the Spirit at His baptism, Jesus fulfills His ministry free from a fleshly fallen nature. He promises us the same life as we die to ourselves, receive His resurrection life and are filled with His Spirit. While we will never be perfect in this life, we will grow moment by moment, day by day.

WHAT JESUS IS FREE FOR

In Jesus we see ourselves as God intends us to be—free. But freedom isn't simply negative: being released from Satan's grip, the world, legalism, money, false values, sin and the flesh. Freedom is also positive. We are set free for God and for each other.

The Love of His Father

Jesus shows His love for the Father by obeying Him. Out of love, He withdraws to a lonely place in the early hours to see the face of the Father. He sustains an intimate relationship by speaking and listening to His Father. This is their love relationship in action. It is out of this same love that Jesus ministers. His works bear witness to His Father, who sent Him.

Because of His love and His intimacy with the Father, Jesus isn't addicted to His ministry or His relationships. Unlike pastoral workaholics, He is free to leave a successful campaign behind and move on to other cities. Motivated by God's call and direction rather than by the needs around Him, He is free to withdraw and find rest and refreshment guilt free.

When an expert in the Law asks Jesus about the greatest commandment, He replies, "'You shall love the Lord your God with all your heart, and with all your soul, and with all your mind.' This is the great and foremost commandment. The second is like it, 'You shall love your neighbor as yourself.' On these two commandments depend the whole Law and the Prophets" (Matt. 22:37-40, *NASB*). This is Jesus' freedom: to love the Father fully and to love us in the same way.

As we walk these 12 steps with Jesus, our sponsor, we will grow in our love for God. The first commandment is not our burden but our delight. As we worship Him, we become like Him. We seek the Father's face, and like Jesus, we express our love to Him. We grow in intimacy, beginning to hear His voice, and in dependency, relying on His Spirit. Like Jesus, we listen for His Word and delight in His will. As we walk with Jesus, our love for Him reveals our love for the Father.

The Love of His Children
Once after having been fired as the pastor of a church, I had no clue about my future. For months I sat in the early morning darkness praying, "Lord, what do you want me to do?" No answer. Finally, as I prayed out loud one day, my voice trailed off, "Lord, what do You want . . . ?" God spoke. If I have ever heard His voice, I heard it then. He simply said, "I want you." This wasn't what I wanted to hear, but this is what I needed (and still need) to hear. I knew it was the Lord; it was the deepest thing He could ever say to me. He alone fills the hole in my soul.

Since Jesus' love for people is totally healthy, He has no addictive attachments to them. Unlike so many Christians today, He doesn't need to collect important people around Him in order to justify His life or shore up His fragile ego. He needs no endorsements from rock stars, Nobel Prize winners, athletes or politicians. Being free *from* people, He is free *for* people. Ordinary people hear Him gladly. He relates to fishermen, revolutionaries, soldiers and slaves. He treats men and women with equal dignity. At Simon the Pharisee's party, He has no problem when a prostitute shows up (see Luke 7:36-50). (What would our friends think if we arranged to talk with a call girl at a local bishop's tea?) He loves to eat with tax collectors and sinners. His enemies accuse Him of being "a glutton and a drunkard" (v. 34). When has that ever happened to us? Unlike the religious Jews, He is happy to travel through hated Samaria and hang out with reprobates. Although He is sent to the lost sheep of Israel, He brings forgiveness and healing even to Gentiles. Tempting scandal, He welcomes women as His disciples. He embraces little children, holding them and blessing them, as a sign of the Kingdom. Farmers, shepherds, babies—these humble people provide the images for His sayings and stories.

Jesus is free to care for all kinds of people. He comforts them, confronts them, responds to their pain and welcomes them into a new life—a new way of being Israel. I heard Dick Halverson, former chaplain to the United States Senate, remark, "Jesus cannot be interrupted since His ministry is His interruptions. His agenda is to identify human need and do what love dictates."[4] Jesus goes beyond the illnesses that usually force us to seek help such as alcoholism or chronic depression. By confronting our core issues, He risks our rejection. His greatest ministry values are our freedom and well-being; therefore, He continues to love a rejecting world. When He teaches us to love our enemies, He is believable (see Matt. 5:44). He signs this demand in His own blood.

Because of Satan's assaults, our fallen world and Jewish political messianic expectations, Jesus knows that He will suffer. He sees Himself as actually bringing division and conflict. His disciples misunderstand Him. His opponents hound Him and plot His death. Judas betrays Him. Peter denies Him. Finally, Jesus offers Himself as a sacrifice on a cross that bridges heaven and Earth. There, as He asks His heavenly Father to forgive His enemies, He is left to bleed and suffocate to death. His love breaks our pride and our hearts. Yet we must know that it is through this suffering that sin is cancelled and Christ's kingdom fully comes.

Jesus' death is the ultimate expression of His freedom to love His neighbor as Himself. All of His acts are acts of love. For love He heals the sick. For love He casts out demons. For love He bears God's wrath, which we deserve. Jesus' love for people is written on every page of the Gospels.

Jesus loves us freely. Since He is our sponsor, He also sets us free to love each other and ourselves. As we receive His mercy and become merciful toward ourselves, we are able to extend mercy to our neighbors. Such love throws us into each other's arms for care and comfort. It enables us to be good news to the world. Since Jesus doesn't condemn us, we must not condemn each other or ourselves. Since He loves His enemies (including us), we must love our enemies (even when our enemy may be our own abusive selves). Since He forgives us, we must forgive each other and ourselves. Since He comes to seek and save the lost, we must seek and save the lost. A Church in love with God and its neighbors fulfills the Great Commission throughout the whole global village. As we mirror Jesus' presence, we live out our new freedom in relationship to the only fully functional person who has ever lived.

I remember when a man named Jimmy found his way into our storefront in San Diego. While he sat in the back, he got to witness some members of Christ's Church loving each other, regardless of ethnicity: Emile, our South African Dutch manager, and his roommate, David, were overcome with emotion as they said good-bye to Oscar, an African-American man who had lived with them for a time. Watching them weep and embrace, Jimmy said to himself, *That's what I want.* A short time later, he became a Christian and began his journey off the streets.

To know the free Jesus is to experience our own freedom. Invaded by His Spirit, we live increasingly spontaneous lives in Him. To know Jesus is to renounce our idols—the relationships, substances and processes to which we are addicted and which enslave us. To know Jesus is to be liberated from the performance demands of our culture. It is to experience heavenly control (our freedom) rather than earthly control (our bondage). It is to unmask Satan's deceptions, ungodly family expectations and the demands of this world system.

Once our relationship with God has been restored and we begin to love Him with all our hearts, our relationships with each other will be restored. Once submitted to Christ's lordship, we will be able to exercise divine rulership over this planet once again. Sin, Satan and disease will be challenged and conquered in the name of Jesus. While we only see partial victory now, we can rest in the assurance that Jesus has already won the battle. We have read the last chapter and everything turns out all right, which frees us spiritually to be relevant to the world in its deepest hunger—its hunger for the living God.

LIVING FREE?

Where are you in this journey? Jesus has come to set you free from everything that steals your true humanity, holds you in an alien grip, leaves you hungover with guilt and shame, and bashes your self-image and self-esteem. The life He has for you is totally positive. You are free *from* in order to be free *for*. God wants to work His love in you so that you can give it away, loving Him in return, loving yourself and loving everyone else around you. If Jesus is in your life, this is happening right now for you. Just accept it; say yes to it. You are in the process of becoming more and more like Him.

- From what has Jesus already set you free?
- From what is Jesus in the process of setting you free?
- What are the bondages in your life that you need to surrender to Him?

- What are the weak points in your character that make you vulnerable to Satan's attacks?
- Invite Jesus to heal the cracks in your character.
- How is Jesus transforming you so that you can be free to love God? How do you express that love to Him?
- What role does worship play in your life?
- How is Jesus transforming you so that you can be free to love yourself?
- How is Jesus transforming you so that you can be free to love those around you?
- How are you doing with loving your enemies?
- Ask Jesus to give you grace and fill you with His love.
- How serious are you about becoming more like Jesus?

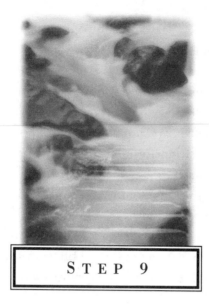

Live Self-Giving with the Self-Giving Jesus

As we have seen, addicts are either users of substances (like alcohol, nicotine and caffeine), people (through dysfunctional relationships) or processes (such as work, sex, gambling or exercise). Addicts also are preoccupied with controlling their sources of supply. Since their disease is progressive, it demands more and more to achieve the same effect. As it is often said, there is no one more selfish than an addict looking for a fix.

Jesus is the alternative to an addictive, consumptive lifestyle. He is self-giving rather than self-taking. He lives loving God and loving people with a proper love for Himself. Jesus, however, doesn't live outside Himself at the expense of His true thoughts or feelings. No false front hides His shame. He doesn't manipulate others in order to gain control over them. He doesn't use "love" to mask rage. He doesn't stop living His own life in order to live someone else's life.

Jesus is not a codependent caregiver, losing Himself in serving others out of low self-esteem. As Melody Beattie writes, "Codependents are reactionaries. They overreact. But rarely do they act."[1] This isn't Jesus. He is always proactive with us in obedience to the Father. He is no victim. He experiences no abandonment. He is able to be naked and unashamed before others. He knows who He is and what He is about. He is the one fully functional person. Because of this, He fearlessly and freely gives Himself away. He will be your sponsor.

THE SELF-GIVING JESUS LOVES US

Jesus shows His self-giving by loving others. He knows that "love" is a verb as well as a noun. It implies action. We must love our neighbor as ourselves. Jesus illustrates this in His story about the good Samaritan (see Luke 10:25-37). Religious leaders are traveling on the treacherous Jericho road. They pass by a man who has been beaten and robbed. They avoid involvement. They don't want to get contaminated. We can imagine their rationalizations: "I'm late for Temple." "When I get to Jerusalem, I'll demand more police protection on this road." "This man is a fool to travel alone. He has gotten what he deserves." "He must have some sin in his life. I'm glad God judged him."

Surprisingly, while the clergy avoid the injured man, the hated, heretical, half-breed Samaritan stops. Taking the initiative, he goes to where the man is. (Here love makes the first move.) Rather than seeing the man out of his peripheral vision, the Samaritan actually sees him. (Love doesn't avoid; it doesn't go into denial. Love sees the crisis for what it is. Love faces the truth.) Having seen the man, the Samaritan feels compassion—his heart is touched. He goes with his gut reaction. (Notice that his feelings come after seeing the victim. They don't lead him. He is led by the reality of the situation.)

Love now goes into action. First, the Samaritan deals with the man's wounds and stops the bleeding. Rather than giving a sermon, he gives first aid. Second, he accepts responsibility for the man's recovery. He puts him on his donkey and takes him to an inn, promising the proprietor that he will cover the bill. Jesus concludes that this is what it means to love our neighbors as ourselves. We are to go and do likewise.

In the deepest sense, the good Samaritan is Jesus. When all others pass by, He stops. When no one glances our way, He sees us. He feels compassion. He binds up our wounds and restores us to health. This is Jesus' kind of love—unconditional, caring for our best interests without any reference to Himself and His needs. He doesn't derive value from us; He invests value in us. When Jesus goes freely to the cross, He never asks, "What's in it for Me?" His only concern is "What's in it for You, Father, and what's in it for them?"

Jesus serves His followers in exactly the same way. During Passover, He lays aside His garments, as He laid aside His glory, and washes His disciples' feet. He loves us and frees us to love in the same way. His disciples call Him master and Lord, and they are right—He is. So if He washes their feet, He puts them and us into the foot-washing business. This is how people know that we belong to Him—we love as He loves (see John 13:35).

As our sponsor, Jesus teaches us how to live self-giving lives. We are to share our goods with those in need. We are to care for the poor and oppressed. We are to lay down our lives for each other. Loving like this is, in the phrase of Reinhold Niebuhr, our "impossible possibility."[2] Only Jesus' love enables us to love each other this way. He prays that "the love you have for me may be in them and that I myself may be in them" (John 17:26). Such servantlike love is radical and will always overturn the world's expectations.

Richard came to our church from Hollywood Boulevard. He was large, unattractive and fearful. He had made sexual advances toward a young man, and when his overtures had not been returned, he had threatened violence. As I got beyond my fears and got to know Richard, I learned that as a young boy he had watched his father kill his mother and then kill himself. As a result, he had been bounced from institution to institution. Landing in Hollywood, he came to know Jesus through our street ministry. Richard received the gift of a simple faith. If it was in the Bible, he believed it. Little by little, leaders in the church rallied to help him. When a landlord threatened to evict him, Bob Toms, then Governor Reagan's commissioner of corporations, became his lawyer. Jim Oraker, a psychologist, became his counselor and helped him handle his rage.

One night we celebrated Richard's birthday. As we held hands and prayed, tears came to my eyes. I looked around the room filled with leaders from our community and church who had gathered to honor Richard. Here was something of the servant heart of Jesus. He says to us:

> You know that those who are regarded as rulers of the Gentiles lord it over them, and their high officials exercise authority over them. Not so with you. Instead, whoever wants to become great among you must be your servant, and whoever wants to be first must be slave of all (Mark 10:42-44).

Why is this? Because "the Son of Man did not come to be served, but to serve, and to give his life as a ransom for many" (v. 45).

In professional ministry, there is not much room at the top, but there is always room at the bottom. No one competed with Mother Teresa years ago when she began caring for the dying on the streets of Calcutta. Just as Jesus gave His life for us, He commands that we go and do likewise.

Jesus not only serves His followers, but He also serves the world. He lavishes His love and power on the demonized, the blind, the lame, the deaf and dumb, the paralyzed and the lepers. He loves those with withered limbs and withered souls. His hands are always outstretched, touching the untouchable. He hears the cries of the sick and dying and answers them.

It was this kind of love that hooked me as an insecure high school sophomore. I had been trapped within myself and fearful of people. Then, some Christians who were leaders in my high school learned my name and took time out for me. They gave me a ride to Tuesday-night fellowship meetings in area homes. They included me in their fun, even though I wasn't any fun. They invited me to the weekend camp where I became a Christian. When I heard that Jesus loves me unconditionally, I could believe it, because I had seen that love in them.

To let the self-giving Jesus sponsor us means that we will give ourselves in love to each other and to the world. There is no other option. As we get out of ourselves and into Him and each other, we will learn how to live as God intended us to live.

THE SELF-GIVING JESUS TELLS US THE TRUTH

In an age of propaganda, image manipulation, spin, public posturing and denial, Jesus is the truth and tells the truth. The addictive culture and addictive Church maintain themselves through nonconfrontational lies and deceit. They are obsessed with control and will sacrifice anything to keep it.

During the 1970s, I served on a national Presbyterian task force studying the ordination of self-affirming, practicing homosexual persons into the ministry. After our committee had met for a short time, it became clear that the task force was a sham. With a large budget and support staff for a several-year process, the outcome had been predetermined. The chairperson and a majority of the committee had been chosen to represent the Church hierarchy's view that gays should be ordained. A token minority made things look fair. Consultations were held across the country so that the Church could create the illusion that the process was open. Experts, such as sex researcher Dr. William Masters of Masters and Johnson, gave the study scientific credibility. But even the author of the majority report had been chosen beforehand. The whole process was a charade.

Later I related my experiences to the president of the Covenant Church. He assured me that he too sometimes used executive privilege to stack the deck. He counseled me, "Include just enough opposition to defuse conflict in order to appear fair. They can ventilate without having real power." Like the rest of the world, too often those in Church leadership keep us confused, powerless and controlled. Appearing to do one thing, they do the opposite. This is addictive behavior. Surrounded by lies, who will tell the truth? Jesus will.

In the Sermon on the Mount, Jesus warns against pretentious piety, raving lust, unforgiveness, anger, revenge, materialism and miracle workers with deceptive hearts (see Matt. 5:1-11). What possible personal benefits could He receive from such confrontational remarks? What popular preacher tells us that it is harder for a camel to pass through the eye of a needle than for a rich man to enter the kingdom of God (see Matt. 19:24)? What does Jesus gain by summoning us to take up our crosses and follow Him to death (see Matt. 16:24)? What advantage does He get from warning against praying long prayers and exhorting people to wash their faces and smile while fasting (see Matt. 6)? What is in it for Jesus when He offends our intellects to expose our hearts, telling us to become like little children to enter the Kingdom (see Matt. 18:3)? His only advantage is that He tells us the truth because He loves us, gives Himself to us and wants us to become like Him. He tells

> *As Jesus heals us and secures us in His love, we are free to be ourselves, free to know what we think, free to know what we feel, free to let the chips fall where they may. It begins to feel good!*

the truth for our advantage rather than for His. What He receives from the Father He delivers to us. We're on His heart, and He serves us in order to make us people of the truth.

As Jesus, who is the truth, sponsors us, we will know the truth and begin to tell the truth ourselves. We won't be able to use secrecy and deception in order to maintain control. We won't be able to cover our selfishness with lies or manipulate people with our distortions. We will no longer be able to protect ourselves behind false fronts, using deceit to mask our fear of exposing our shame base. As Jesus heals us and secures us in His love, we are free to be ourselves. We are free to know what we think. We are free to know what we feel. We are free to let the chips fall where they may. It begins to feel good! This is the work of the self-giving Jesus in us.

THE SELF-GIVING JESUS RELEASES HIS POWER

Along with loving us and telling us the truth, Jesus releases His power in us. After the Holy Spirit anoints Jesus for His ministry, He is thrust out into the wilderness to do battle with the devil (see Matt. 4:1). Victorious, Jesus is filled with the Spirit again and is launched into His public ministry. Jesus confirms the work of the Spirit as He reads from the Isaiah scroll in the synagogue in Nazareth:

> The Spirit of the Lord is on me, because he has anointed me to preach good news to the poor. He has sent me to proclaim freedom for the prisoners and recovery of sight for the blind, to release the oppressed, to proclaim the year of the Lord's favor (Luke 4:18-19).

Jesus then comments, "Today this scripture is fulfilled in your hearing" (v. 21). He makes it clear that He hasn't come to form a new religion or run a reform movement. Instead, He fulfills Isaiah's prophecy and the Spirit's promptings to help the poor, the sick and the oppressed. He will meet human need wherever He finds it. With the Spirit's power upon Him and surging through Him, He touches the sick and they are healed. No wonder people press in to hear Jesus. As Francis MacNutt says, "If you want to start a worldwide movement, just heal a few people."[3] Jesus did both through the Spirit's power.

When Jesus speaks His healing word, the blind see and the lame walk. He is the doctor and Israel is His patient load. He comes not for the well but for the sick. He heals by the power of the Spirit, and He does so not without personal cost. He expends time and energy. Crowds harass Him. He gets tired. He moves into the pain, the stink and the stench of broken people. Jesus carries our sorrows in His heart as He extends His hands to pull us from the fire. He finally bears our sins in His own body on the tree.

Power and sacrifice, power and suffering, power and self-giving—this is real Christianity. Knowing this, Jesus says to His followers, "In this world you will have trouble. But take heart! I have overcome the world" (John 16:33). Paul echoes this when he tells the Romans that we also "rejoice in our sufferings" (5:3); and he reminds the Thessalonians, "You became imitators of us and of the Lord; in spite of severe suffering, you welcomed the message with the joy given by the Holy Spirit" (1 Thess. 1:6). The self-giving Jesus promises to minister His power through us; but as it did for Him, such ministry will cost us everything.

Throughout Church history, the coming of the Spirit in power always sparks revival. While this is familiar in Pentecostal and charismatic circles, it has been the heartbeat of historic Christianity long before the last 100 years. John Wesley wrote about an experience six months after his conversion:

Mr. Hall, Hinching, Ingham, Whitefield, Hutching, and my brother Charles were present at our love feast in Fetter Lane with about sixty of our brethren. About three in the morning as we were continuing instant in prayer, the power of God came mightily upon us, insomuch that many cried out for exulting joy and many fell to the ground. As soon as we were recovered a little from the awe and amazement at the presence of His Majesty, we broke out with one voice, "We praise Thee O God, we acknowledge Thee to be the Lord."[4]

It was the Wesleys, Whitefield and others who exploded the Evangelical Awakening in England and the American colonies, changing the face of the English-speaking world to this day.

The famous nineteenth-century evangelist Dwight L. Moody had a similar Spirit encounter. While raising funds to rebuild his church, which had been lost in the Chicago Fire, he found a hunger for the filling of the Holy Spirit:

> My heart was not in the work of begging. . . . I could not appeal. I was crying all the time that God would fill me with His Spirit. Well, one day, in the city of New York—oh, what a day!—I cannot describe it, I seldom refer to it; it is almost too sacred an experience to name. . . . I can only say that God revealed Himself to me, and I had such an experience of His love that I had to ask Him to stay His hand. I went to preaching again. The sermons were not different; I did not present new truths, and yet hundreds were converted. I would not now be placed back where I was before that blessed experience if you should give me all the world—it would be as small dust of the balance.[5]

Moody was a man who had been changed by the self-giving Jesus. Jesus' love and power had been released in him. His ministry was never the same.

What is true for past generations is true today. A new release of the Spirit's power will resuscitate Church life as it did in the book of Acts. We will see fervent evangelism, healing and deliverance; bold intercession; a new hunger for teaching and transparent community. We will be filled with an awesome sense of God's holiness and love in our midst. And we will take this to the world.

THE SELF-GIVING JESUS INVESTS IN US

Jesus not only gives us His love, truth and power, but He also invests His life in us and for us. When He gathers His apostles, He symbolically reconstitutes the 12 tribes of Israel. Beyond this, Jesus calls His followers to be with Him in intimate communion. Like a rabbi who trains his disciples in the Law by what he says and does, so Jesus trains His followers in the same way. They see Him eat. They watch Him sleep. They hear Him pray. After they receive His teaching, they pepper Him with questions in private. Through all of this, He trains them to be the extensions of Himself in the world. He gives them His Word and shows them His works, expecting them to speak and do the same. He teaches them to preach the kingdom of God, heal the sick and cast out demons. He is their model for their ministry. They learn by being in intimate communion with Him. No wonder they turn their world upside down. They become more and more functional as they relate to the functional Jesus. He invests Himself in them, and He invests Himself for them. This costs Him everything.

Jesus fulfills His self-giving love by going to the cross. Cross jewelry and church altars blunt the harshness of His death. We no longer hear the crunch of nailed bones and painful cries. We no longer smell the stench of blood. We no longer see the deformed body. We no longer watch life drain away. Jesus is God's perfect sacrifice, bleeding like a slain lamb, bearing both taunts and transgressions. Jesus knows that all authority is His, but He uses it to wash feet and wash away our sins. Here, indeed, is the one fully self-giving person, the likes of which the world has never known.

Jesus has no all-consuming addiction. He is a receiver and a giver. He receives the Father's presence in intimate communion. He receives the Father's purpose, which gives direction to His mission. He receives the Spirit's anointing power, and then He gives it all away.

Jesus returns the Father's love and gives us His presence and purpose. As the God-Man, Jesus brings the Father to us, and us to the Father. Through His Incarnation, He restores our fallen humanity. He is what we have been made to be and become. Through Him we learn to live fearlessly, freely and selflessly. As the one truly functional person, He alone heals our addictions and codependency. He alone tears off our masks and exposes the fear and shame behind them. But as He does this, He does not destroy us. Rather, He fills the hole in the soul with Himself and recovers our true humanity. He alone heals our "being wound," securing us to the Father who has made us for Himself. He takes us to His heart forever. Jesus is Lord and Savior. Make Him your sponsor.

- How have you experienced the self-giving Jesus in your life?
- How do you know that He loves you?
- How is He continuing to serve you?
- In what areas of your life do you see yourself reflecting His servant love?
- How has Jesus told you the truth?
- How does Jesus tell you the truth?
- How free are you to tell the truth to others?
- Have you experienced the power of the Spirit in your life?
- Ask Jesus to pour His love into your heart by His Spirit.
- Ask Jesus to fill you with His Spirit.

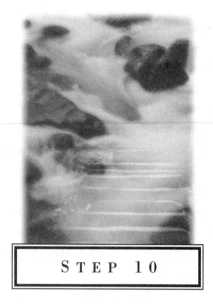

Step into Spiritual Disciplines

As we have seen, after the crisis of conversion, there is the process of growing in Christ. After the crisis of breaking denial, there is the process of withdrawing from addictions and refocusing ourselves on worshiping and loving God. After the crisis of brokenness, there is the process of God's putting us back together again. After the crisis of the Spirit's having come in power, there is the process of growing in His gifts. Our processes will be punctuated by further crises as we follow Jesus. There will be new invasions of God's Spirit and potential relapses back into addiction. It takes time to detox and repattern our craving brains.

Throughout this journey, the goal remains clear. We are to become like our sponsor, Jesus. How exactly, though, does this happen?

Bookstores are filled with manuals on discipleship. Every church has its special approach to spiritual maturity. Rick Warren offers Saddleback Church his book *The Purpose-Driven Life*, a best-selling pathway to maturity in Christ. Much of the available material focuses on building our faith, informing our minds with biblical truth and leading us into obedience. But basically discipleship isn't a program. It's a relationship centered on Jesus—the only fully functional person. It's also a healthy relationship with others in a community. Rather than being sterile and burdensome, the disciplines of the Christian life are liberating, freeing us to relate to Jesus and each other in healthy ways.

To fully become Jesus' disciples, we must allow Him to probe into the depths of our beings. He exposes our craving brains that have been fed by the craving culture. He exposes our generational, environmental and personal sins. As He does this, we are ready to receive His forgiveness and healing. Otherwise, we go through life carrying our past pain and inflicting it on others. True discipleship is built on our dying to our false selves and our attachments, shedding the fear and shame that bind us and rejecting the poisonous pedagogy that compounds our addictions and codependency. The result? We become holy, the whole people God created us to be—set apart to worship Him, become like Him and represent Him in this world.

Discipleship isn't formless piety. The Bible gives us substantial teaching, exhortation, correction and examples of godly living and mutual ministry. How can we find an effective road to healing that embraces a biblical model but isn't legalistic? One time-honored answer comes from the Twelve-Step program of Alcoholics Anyonymous (A.A.).

These simple A.A. directives are rooted in an evangelical Christian context. Behind them is the ministry of Frank Buchman who was converted at the Keswick Convention in England in 1908.[1] After leading substantial student ministries, Buchman founded the Oxford Group as a renewal movement. He stressed the importance of new birth, complete surrender to God's will, confession of sin to one or more persons privately and restitution of wrongs wherever possible. A believer could only remain a true Christian, then, by bringing change to others. Buchman's principles had a direct influence on the founders of A.A. No wonder that in the early years Jesus was the higher power who alone could set the alcoholic free. However, after a huge influx of addicts from all walks of life, the reference to Jesus was dropped. When we restore Him to the center of the Twelve Steps and make Him our sponsor, the Twelve Steps are our pathway to healing and freedom.

The purpose behind the Twelve Steps is to help alcoholics and other addicts surrender to God.[2] Then they are held accountable for the rest of their lives. Since the Christian life is a relationship and not just rules, these steps only help us to grow if we keep Jesus at the center of our lives.

The weakness of the Twelve Steps is their implied moralism and the oversimplification of personal responsibility. We need to add other issues to the mix, such as our genetic inheritance, craving brains and dysfunctional families. We also need to see the power of Jesus' cross in our forgiveness and the power of His Spirit in our transformation—with this in mind, the Twelve Steps have lasting value in aiding in our recoveries from addiction and codependency. Let's take a fresh look at the first seven steps.

STEP ONE

"We admitted we were powerless over alcohol [add your other issues]—that our lives had become unmanageable." According to the original A.A. guidebook, this is the first step to recovery. We painfully confess that our addictions, whether to substances, processes or relationships, are no longer working for us. Pretending to be in control, we are out of control. Our supposed freedom is bogus. As Dr. Rick Whitehill, a psychologist friend of mine, once said, "When I became a Christian, I gave up the illusion of control." We must make a similar surrender, even if it includes indescribable suffering and agony. We abandon the last defense of our independent egos. We renounce self-idolatry that goes back to the Garden of Eden. Our false selves are exposed for what they are—false! Destruction precedes reconstruction. The false self must die. When Jesus confronts us, provoking our surrender, we must give up our addictive attachments. Gerald May points out that we don't lose the objects of our attachments as much as we lose the attachments themselves.[3] We lose the strength of our behavior that made gods out of these objects. In surrender, we may feel fearful, courageous and grace filled all at the same time. Perhaps our biggest fear is that when we admit our powerlessness and give up our attachments, there will be nothing left but the hole in the soul. Remember that we are only at step one. God will use our surrender to come into our lives and fill us with Himself.

Our admission of powerlessness usually comes through crisis. We hit bottom—sometimes with a bounce and sometimes with a crash. For alcoholics or drug addicts, this may come in a planned intervention. A group of family and friends gather on cue to confront us with our behavior and its consequences. Caught in this loving crunch, denial is usually broken, fear is exposed, and change becomes possible. We also may come to our powerlessness through the death of a loved one, the loss of a job, the end of a relationship, a divorce or an illness. A crisis also may come during a conversion when God literally stops us in our tracks.

The crisis of our powerlessness is truly biblical. Pride separates us from God in Eden. Pride seduced our first parents, promising them control over life "like God" (Gen. 3:5). Pride leads us to abandon Him and attach ourselves to the objects of our addictions. But God resists the proud and gives grace to the humble (see 1 Pet. 5:5). He will have a Day of Judgment against all arrogance (see Isa. 2:11). When this pride is broken, then healing begins. This is why Jesus tells us that we must become like little children to enter the Kingdom. Our powerlessness prepares us to receive God's power. Our unmanageable lives prepare us for God's management. Giving up control allows our gnawing inner fears to begin to dissipate.

In step one, God breaks our self-righteousness. As in Jesus' story of the prodigal son, He exposes the elder brother's presumptions, judgments and secret rage. As we take this step, we give up our works of the Law and the spiritual pride that goes with them. Where will that leave us? On our faces, mumbling that we are powerless and that even our religious lives are unmanageable. On our faces, admitting our codependent service to others and our rescue of others to hide the emptiness inside. On our faces, admitting our attachments to drugs, money, food, sex, relationships, work and our own self-image. These are our idols, which prevent the living God from coming into our lives. The first step is the path to healing. We take it with guts and grace.

I admitted my own powerlessness in the crisis of my conversion. I realized how much Jesus loves me and how I share responsibility for His death. My heart was broken. I knew that I could no longer manage my life. Another crisis came when my wife, Kathryn, and I, in deep emotional pain, admitted that we were powerless over our relationship. Years later, I was broken again when I was fired as a pastor. Now I was powerless over my church. I had been separated from my "drug" and my codependent relationships. Numb and depressed, I retreated into myself with my shattered dreams. These crises were God's severe mercy and my first step to healing. All of us will go through crises as God brings down our idols and sets us free to love Him. Acknowledging that we are out of control is the first step to becoming like the fearless Jesus.

STEP TWO

"[We] came to believe that a power greater than ourselves could restore us to sanity." Step two implies that our addictions have made us insane. Now we have a choice—life or death. For the alcoholic or drug addict, the choice is physically real. Many of my chemically addicted friends saw their insanity as they courted death by overdosing. Other addictions and codependences perpetuate the illusion of life, while being just as deadly.

The second step opens with "[we] came to believe." Belief is the issue after we admit our powerlessness. We can give in to faith or despair. Once denial has been broken and we admit to our false selves, with all our addictions and fears, we will either die (quickly or slowly) or seek help beyond ourselves. But where can we find it? Not in this world.

Apart from Jesus, everyone else is as insane as we are, and the inmates run the asylum. We are all addicts. We all mask shame behind proper costumes and false selves. Why should we entrust our lives to this addicted world and its ideologies? Can the blind lead the blind? Clearly, we need a "power greater than ourselves." We need a power greater than any self-help group. We don't need another codependent rescuer. This power can't be another addiction. This power is God alone—the only One who will never abandon us regardless of how lost or lonely we feel. He doesn't want to be an addiction. As Gerald May says, God will not allow Himself to become another object of our attachment, "because . . . [God] desires full love, not addiction."[4]

The God of the Bible dwells in unapproachable light. He is holy and sovereign over the world He created. He is the awesome judge who holds us accountable for our lives. He is also the loving Father who sent His Son to redeem us and bring us home. Jesus, who has conquered the devil, sin and death, now reigns over the universe. He is in the place of authority, at the Father's right hand.

> *Acknowledging that we are out of control is the first step to becoming like the fearless Jesus.*

One day all things will be consummated in His glorious return. He is the "power greater than ourselves." He is no abstraction. He is a trustworthy person who bears eternal, unconditional love from the Father's heart to ours. He restores our relationship with God. Our abandonment is gone. We cry, "Abba! Father!" As we open our hearts to Him, He comes in through His Spirit (see Rom. 8:9).

The living God is the power that restores us to sanity. The only question is Do I believe this? If we are stuck here, we need to pray, "God, give me the faith to believe that through Jesus You are the power greater than myself and that You alone can heal me." He answers this prayer as we keep praying from our surrendered, unmanageable hearts. We begin to sense that Jesus is here for us too. Faith begins to replace fear. This is the next step in becoming like the fearless Jesus.

STEP THREE

"[We] made a decision to turn our will and our lives over to the care of God as we understood Him." This God is often called a higher power. At best, this is vague. What is "God as we understood him"? Anything or anyone can be this god: an A.A. group, any religious experience, a therapist, a pastor, a guru or even a new addiction. Many alcoholics have said in A.A. open meetings, "My sponsor is my higher power." Originally, step three encouraged surrender to Jesus as Lord. He is the Savior, not as we understand Him, but as He understands Himself and makes Himself known to us. Confronted by Him, we are called to become accountable for our lives. He is King. Will we submit to Him? He is Lord. Will we serve Him? He is Savior. Will we receive Him? He is our sponsor. Once we give up being our own god, we must meet Jesus on His terms rather than ours. A more appropriate step three would be "We made a decision to turn our will and our lives over to the care of God as He is revealed in His Son, the Lord Jesus Christ."

The third step calls us to surrender our wills. Jesus doesn't break our wills with poisonous pedagogy. He doesn't beat us until we give up. On the contrary, He takes the punishment we deserve. Out of undying love, He woos us, drawing us to Himself. Through His acts of mercy, He crushes our hard hearts and fills them with Himself. This goes to the core of our being and our shame base is shattered. We are no longer abandoned. We are forgiven. We begin to heal. Jesus comes into our hearts. This is the miracle of new birth in Christ Jesus.

Psychologically, as we give our desires and cravings to Christ, we detach from the objects of our addictions. We repent of our idols, stop our addictive behaviors and go through the stress of withdrawal. Now we are set free to love God and our neighbors as ourselves. If you are like me, addicted to work and people, this detachment requires grace. Since I became addicted to the Church, God separated me physically from it more than once. Years ago, He clearly told me to resign one position. Then later He had me fired from another. He has worked on me through the pain, wedding my heart to Himself again, freeing me to love Him with all I have. We must separate or be separated from our addictive attachments. This allows us to love in freedom rather than from compulsion.

According to step three, when we give our wills and our lives over to Jesus, He receives them. He claims them and renews them for His kingdom. This leads to total renovation.

If Jesus offers us boundless freedom, what keeps us from the surrender called for in step three? First, we may fear that if we give Him our lives, we will be abused. He will make us become missionaries in remote parts of the world, and we'll hate it. If we come home drunk, He will be angry. Dark pictures of a vengeful or vindictive Jesus haunt some of us. Some because they have been wounded by abusive priests, pastors or Sunday School teachers who represented Jesus out of their own anger, fear or lust. Others because they keep a guilt-centered relationship with Him, only knowing the crucified Jesus. But He is also the risen Jesus. He throws a welcome home party for us and promises that nothing can separate us from His love (see Rom. 8:38-39).

As our sponsor, Jesus takes total responsibility for our lives. As He graces us to face our childhood abuse issues head-on and pray over them, restoration begins. Why then would He inflict more pain on us? To surrender to anything or anyone less than Jesus is to surrender to another addictive idol. We simply become cross-addicted, exchanging one tyrannical addiction for another; and to our horror, we discover that we will be abused again. But to surrender to Jesus is to fall into the arms of the loving Father. Like the prodigal son, we come home to His house and get the family ring, new clothes and the fattened calf. It's party time!

Second, we may resist surrender because we're unwilling to go through withdrawals. Separating ourselves from addictive attachments can result in more stress, unsatisfied cravings, depression and disorientation. We must be prepared realistically for this. Sometimes, when God comes, all we feel is incredible joy. It is the "honeymoon" period. But the battle isn't over. The devil is an active enemy who contests each work of God. The fallen world, relationship conflicts, unbalanced brain chemistry and our survival instincts may all trigger cravings that demand to be satisfied.

WHERE TO GO FROM HERE

Once God intervenes in our lives decisively, the healing begins. We must daily admit that we are powerless. We must daily give over our wills to God. We must daily believe that only He can keep us sane. We must daily find our strength in Jesus. A.A. teaches that we must turn our addictions over daily, hourly or minute by minute. Once we make this initial commitment and Jesus has our car keys, bank accounts, address books, charge cards, Internet access, hunger, partying, families, self-image and codependent relationships, we are ready to move on to step four. Delivered from our addictions, we begin to be delivered from our fears. We can then begin to live with the fearless Jesus. We will mirror Him more and more. We begin to get free with the free Jesus.

STEP FOUR

"[We] made a searching and fearless moral inventory of ourselves." Jesus frees us from the past. This includes bondage to Satan, this world system (including family control, legalism and fear of scarcity), sin, the Law and the flesh, namely, our false front masking our shame-based lives. As we make our "searching and fearless moral inventory," specifics will surface. This includes the hurts we have inflicted on others as well as the hurts that have been inflicted on us.

Search

For starters, we must set aside serious time by ourselves. We need to hear God's voice in silence, uncorrupted by the chatter of this world. We need quiet meditation. We need to remember our past. We must honestly face our family relationships. How were they dysfunctional? What was our place in them? What roles did we play? Did we grow or merely survive? Go back to your childhood and ask Jesus to penetrate any denial or rationalization covering up your past. Significant memory lapse probably means that we're blocking unacknowledged pain and abuse. Professional therapists, pastoral counselors or mature friends can help us recover lost years. The fourth step says that our inventory must be "searching." Keeping a private journal may help. Ask Jesus to shine His light on every dark spot. He is with you through it all.

While we strive for honesty, we guard against perfectionism. We need not uncover and uproot everything. Timing is important. God never shows us more than we can handle. Grace covers all the sin and abuse in our lives. But we need to be conscious of key personal and moral issues. We need to expose the memory blocks that have kept us wounded. Pray, "Lord, help me to remember what I need to know now. Bring other things to mind when I am ready and in your time."

Don't Fear

Our inventory also must be "fearless." We need to try to see things as they really are and not as our parents told us they were, or as we rationalize things to be. Only the fearless and gracious Jesus can help us to do this boldly. He is our sponsor. He will guide us through the process.

The fourth step exposes the perversion of our thoughts as well as our actions. We must face the damage we've done to our parents and family out of rebellion. Our inventory will include the people that we have used, abused and rejected. We will face our sexual sins, exploits, conquests, seductions and adulteries—both of heart and behavior.

We need to catalog any false religions in which we have participated, such as Satanism, Mormonism, Jehovah's Witnesses, Buddhism, ESP, TM or various New Age religions. Our inventories must include any contact we may have had with the occult or witchcraft. This means even "innocent" things such as palm readings, astrology or Ouija boards. We need to repent of all contacts, renounce all spiritual connections and receive Jesus' forgiveness for them.

Our inventories also need to include all addictive issues. What were our parents' addictions? How have they been role models for us? How have we used alcohol or drugs? How have we used sex, exercise or food? What have our close friendships looked like? What is our sexual history? We need to recall those with whom we went to school, worked and socialized, those whom we dated and those whom we lived near. How have we handled even casual encounters? Who have we cheated and used? Are we perfectionists? Are we judgmental? Are we controlling? How have we manipulated others and people pleased? We need to spell this out clearly. We have been hooked by many addictions. We have also willfully participated in them by worshiping our idols and feeding our fantasies. We have lived in the illusion that we can control our addictions, but they have controlled us. We've promised again and again that we will quit tomorrow. This makes us insane.

Examine

Next, we need to examine our false selves—our life in the flesh. What have we used to deceive people? How have we hidden our true selves, emotions, desires and longings? What images have we fostered? What spin have we used? What are our fears? Of what are we ashamed?

In our "searching and fearless moral inventory," we need to know how others have hurt us. As we look at our past, we find that we have not only sinned against people but that they also have sinned against us. While I admit rebellion against my parents, I also need to admit their poisonous pedagogy. Healing includes addressing the pain that has been inflicted on us. Addictions often are generational. I've inherited some of my addictions and codependences from my family. If a parent is an alcoholic, then the child is a codependent, and that is that. My friend's father is a workaholic and an alcoholic. He is also a Christian and an elder in his church. His son became an alcoholic and a sexual addict. When the son finally received treatment, he discovered generations of abuse that had been transmitted through his father. In recovery, the addictive chain was broken.

Beyond family relationships, I have had to deal with friends, classmates, coaches, teachers, employers, pastors and lay leaders who have rejected me, judged me, manipulated me, abused me, deceived me and kept me in fear.

STEP FIVE

"[We] admitted to God, to ourselves, and to another human being the exact nature of our wrongs [and the wrongs committed against us]."

Confess Sin to God

Moral inventory leads us to confession. This sets us free from guilt and bondage. We become free like the free Jesus and learn to live free in Him. We confess our wrongdoings to God, because they violate His moral will. We are lawbreakers in His ordered universe. Since He created us, He knows what is best for us. When we exhibit self-righteousness, pride, greed and anger; when we lie, steal or indulge in sexual sin; when we make addictive attachments; we not only hurt others and ourselves, we hurt God. Through sin we deny that He is God. We do not love Him freely. We reject His plan and purpose for His creation and for us. When we admit to God "the exact nature of our wrongs," we are no longer captive to guilt and shame. We not only admit our sins, but we also give ourselves to God and recover our right relationship with Him through the death of His Son. We ask Him to send a wave of cleansing through our hearts. When we confess our sins, God not only sets us free from the past, but He also frees us for the future filled with the adventure of serving Him in this world.

Most of us live with unconfessed sin. We limp through life with a load of guilt, hiding behind our false selves. This perpetuates dishonesty, spiritual pride and deep loneliness. No one really knows us. We break shame as we confess our sins one step at a time and present our moral inventory to God in reflection and prayer.

Confess Sin to Each Other

Christians also are to confess their sins to each other. James says that if a person is sick he or she should call the elders (see 5:14). The elders are to anoint the person with oil and pray. All sins will be forgiven. (Any link between sickness and sin will be broken.) James concludes:

> Therefore confess your sins to each other and pray for each other so that you may be healed. The prayer of a righteous man [or woman] is powerful and effective (v. 16).

Now, through confession, we detach from that which holds our hearts captive. This breaks our sinful entanglements and frees us to turn to our loving God with all that we are. Pray this simple prayer:

In Jesus' name I confess [state your wrongdoing] *as sin
and ask You, heavenly Father, to forgive me and cleanse
me with the blood of Your Son.*

As we admit our wrongs to God, we admit them to ourselves at
the same time. But we cannot stop there.

To complete this process, we need to find one or two non-
judgmental, mature Christian friends who will hear our confession. Like us, they must be broken. They also need to experience
God's forgiveness and healing. They need to be committed to
absolute confidentiality. Together, then, each item in our inventory will be addressed and released. They might use this formu-
la step by step: "In Jesus' name, I pronounce God's forgiveness
for the sin of [state your wrongdoing]. I break the power of guilt
and shame in your life in Jesus' name. Amen!"

For many of us to admit "the exact nature of our wrongs"
to another person is difficult and even may be offensive. We
may balk at this because it's embarrassing and humiliating to
let others know the secrets of our hearts. It also raises the questions Can I really trust these people? Will they protect me? Will
they bring what they know about me back up again later? Will
they think less of me? If we don't confess our sins to each
other, we miss a central way for God to heal us. And the silence
kills us.

Jesus often makes His intercession and mercy effective
through people. As we confess, our hypocrisy and our hiding
melt. We are no longer "religious." We are real. True Christians
extend love and mercy to our brokenness and tears. Confession
also protects us from excessively spiritualizing our temptations.
We can't blame everything on the devil. We make our own con-
tributions.

Some years ago, I became obsessed with a particular sexual
fantasy. It plagued me and held me captive. Finally, I confessed

it to my best friend at the time. He heard my pain and prayed for me. This broke the fantasy's power. It never returned. Years later, after he had crossed the boundaries of his marriage into sexual sin, we sat at the beach as he unburdened his heart to me. This began his journey to ending an affair and restoring his marriage. It also started his healing from lifelong depression that he had medicated through his driving lust.

We need to hear God's promise, "If we confess our sins, he is faithful and just and will forgive us our sins and purify us from all unrighteousness" (1 John 1:9). We need to know that God hears and answers us again and again. He never says, "I'm sick and tired of that one," or "Not that one again." We also need the faith of trusted friends to help us to stand in grace.

Our confession is not simply to an anonymous priest in a cathedral booth. We confess to someone who can make a similar confession to us. We must guard ourselves against self-righteous people or even well-meaning people who stab us with criticism in the form of good advice. Jesus' word to the woman taken in adultery is His word to us: "Neither do I condemn you. . . . Go now and leave your life of sin" (John 8:11). As I mentioned, the friend who heard my confession was later able to trust me with his. As we support each other, Jesus heals us.

Self-disclosure breeds intimacy. Trusted friends who hear our confessions also keep us accountable. At an addiction seminar in England recently, two university students shared their journey into intimacy. They had decided to become accountable to each other for the sexual temptations in their lives. The first time they had shared all of this together was the hardest. Once their cards were on the table, they met weekly. This supported their commitment to give up pornography and its consequences. They not only strengthened each other and guarded each other, they also bonded with each other. They resolved to be godly men.

Forgive Others' Sin

Since God forgives us, we must forgive those who wrong us. Our Sunday prayer, "Forgive us our debts [or sins, or trespasses], as we also have forgiven our debtors" (Matt. 6:12), mocks us if we don't live it out. For example, if workaholic or alcoholic parents abused us, we need to forgive them. If we hold on to our anger to keep power over them, we live in unforgiveness. This ultimately only hurts us. Jesus brings forgiveness and freedom. As we forgive our abusers, our anger or revenge no longer controls us. We experience the deep truth of Jesus: The forgiven forgive.

Once we forgive, we are ready to grieve our losses. This includes breaking through denial and releasing anger and sorrow. If we avoid this process, we will be emotional cripples. As Alice Miller says, "It is [the] . . . lack of hope of ever being able to express repressed traumata by means of relevant feelings that most often causes severe psychological problems."[5] Unexpressed grief leaves our "inner child" emotionally stunted. John Bradshaw adds that many of us need help finishing our "unresolved grief from childhood—grief resulting from abandonment, abuse in all forms, the neglect of childhood developmental dependency needs, and the enmeshments that result from family-system dysfunction."[6] We must ask God to help us experience our emotional pains before we can let them go.

One friend told me of the horror of lying in bed and hearing his drunken father pull the belt out of his pants as he came down the hallway to beat him. No wonder he refuses to sleep alone. What is the way out for him? He must grieve the loss of his father's protection and love that he deserved as a child. He needs to weep over the irrational punishment that brought him such terror. He also needs to admit his anger toward his dad, forgive him for the abuse and forgive himself for harboring bitterness and resentment in his heart. As he does this, the wounds will heal. They need not be passed on to his children. The generational chain can be broken. His freedom will set others free.

My own childhood grief surfaced when I realized how my dad's absence during World War II had wounded me. I pictured myself at four years of age watching him leave and found myself weeping for the loss he must have felt. Then I heard a little

> *Confession is not only good for the soul, but it is also another step toward being free like our sponsor Jesus.*

child's voice inside of me crying, "Daddy, why did you have to go? I needed you so much." With this, 50 years of buried pain burst out. I wept and wept. The abandonment and shame that I had felt began to dissipate. As I forgave my dad, I also forgave myself for all the years of unconscious anger and fear. Because of my grieving and Jesus' comfort, my stress over abandonment is less of an issue now. I have a more secure sense of myself in Him.

When we challenge fear, we are free to face our sins and pain before God and each other. Confession is not only good for the soul, but it is also another step toward being free like our sponsor Jesus. He alone liberates us from our past bondages, enabling us to love God fully and to love our neighbors as ourselves.

STEP SIX

"[We] were entirely ready to have God remove all these defects of character." It's one thing to confess our sins. It's another thing to want to be free from them. After all, they work for us and their emotional hooks leave us vulnerable. It's one thing to confess our lust. It's another to want to be free from consuming sexual passion and pornographic fantasy. To be free, we must detach ourselves from the "drug" of mood-altering sexual arousal. To be free we must get behind the lust to the anger, loneliness or depression it masks. We must deal with the perversion in our craving brains. We also must remove ourselves from the situations in which we associate lust with destructive behaviors and instead channel our desire toward loving God.

After confession, we must answer Jesus' question to the lame man by the pool of Bethesda: "Do you want to get well?" (John 5:6). If we answer yes we are ready to move on to repentance and its benefits. It means that we are ready for God to change us. To repent means to reverse course—we move toward God instead of away from Him. This is not moralistic or legalistic. This doesn't mean that we are ready to change ourselves; rather, we are ready for God "to remove all these defects of character." His intervention and grace alone set us free.

Notice that step six says we are "entirely ready." This means that we have hit bottom and confessed our powerlessness in step one. With disgust, we have seen through sin's deception. We know that our moral failures and addictions will no longer work for us. In despair over our lives, we cry out to God to change us.

STEP SEVEN

"[We] humbly asked Him [God] to remove our shortcomings." This step goes beyond confession. It asks God to change us. It starts with repentance and leads to detachment from the objects of our cravings. "Repent" in the Old Testament means "to turn." We turn from our sins. We turn to God. We turn from self-will to His will. He is the only One worthy of our worship, passion and desire. He is the only One worthy of our love and delight.

In step four, we faced ourselves squarely. In step five, we confessed our sins and received God's forgiveness. Now our prayer is to turn from these sins and by His grace not feed them again. If we are alcoholics, we quit drinking. If we are codependents, we quit using people.

Our turning also involves surrendering the perceived benefits of our addictions. If we are having an affair, the benefits may include companionship, excitement, sexual gratification, avoidance of a difficult marriage and false comfort for a midlife crisis. We renounce these benefits in Jesus' name and grieve their absence.

We also ask God to heal us from whatever past abuse has contributed to our immoralities and craving brains. The sense of God's absence, generational sin and poisonous pedagogy have all enlarged the hole that we've tried to fill with our addictions. Along the way, we've lied to others and ourselves. Now we are ready for God to change us. We ask Him to remove our shortcomings and heal our vulnerable points.

We may pray, *Break my pride; make me humble. Break my addictions; set me free. Break my lying; make me honest.* We keep praying this until we feel relief. Then we ask for God's Spirit to heal our "being wound" and fill us with Himself. His presence penetrates our shame-based lives. We are abandoned no more. God loves us. God accepts us. We are His. We are no longer worthless and alone, bouncing around in a meaningless universe. His Son has come for us and holds us in His strong grip.

We pray for wholeness—to become more like Jesus, our sponsor. *Jesus, make me fearless like You. Jesus, make me free like You.* Our prayers agree with God's purpose to repopulate this planet with images of Himself. Now we are ready to give ourselves away.

TAKE A LOOK AT YOURSELF

At this point, we need to assimilate our steps. Where are we in the crisis? Have we reached the conviction that our lives are unmanageable? Do we see the insanity in our behaviors? Can we admit that we are out of control? Are we ready for God's control?

- Take the time to reflect on these first seven steps.
- Which one applies to your life right now?
- Which one do you tend to pass over?
- Which one threatens you?
- Which one makes the most sense to you?
- Reflect on the sequence of the steps. See yourself walking down this path.
- Have you given yourself to Jesus as the only higher power?
- Will you give yourself to Him again, day by day?
- Have you done your moral inventory? What has been difficult or painful for you?
- Who in your life can join you as you confess your sins? If you don't know that person, ask God to bring him or her into your life.
- Have you actually sat down and gone over your inventory with another person? If not, what is keeping you from doing so? How will you deal with this?
- Have you received God's full forgiveness? The fact is that He forgives you in Jesus. Do you feel that fact? Ask Him to make this real in your guts.
- Have you asked God to fill the hole in your soul with His Spirit? What is the result of that prayer?
- What shortcomings have you asked God to remove? Where are you in this process?

STEP 11

Continue the Work

Why does God release us from our fears and set us free? First, because He loves us and wants us to be whole. Second, because He wants us to become self-giving like Himself. When we love like Jesus, our self-fulfillment is a by-product. But how can we give ourselves away? Giving up fear and entering into freedom mean steps eight to twelve become our trustworthy guides. Remember, the Christian life is crisis and process. While God throws us into crisis again and again, the process over a lifetime is to become more like Jesus.

STEP EIGHT

"[We] made a list of all persons we had harmed, and became willing to make amends to them all." Like our inventory in step four, this step requires reflection and prayer. We ask God to break through our denial and rationalizations. We ask Him to expose the damage we have done to others. A drug addict might ask: Whom have I stolen from in order to get my drugs? Whom have I lied to about my using? Whom have I hurt by my emotional absence? Whom have I abused when I was high? Whom have I turned on to drugs? and Who has stayed up all night waiting for me to come home?

It's more difficult to believe that we've harmed others in our codependent relationships. Since we are no longer in denial, we can see how we've operated in unhealthy ways. A relational addict needs to ask: Whom have I lied to out of fear? When have I avoided confrontation? Whom have I "helped" to control the relationship for my own benefit? How have I used people to win their approval? and How has my flattery reinforced their false selves?

As our list of people grows, we must be "willing to make amends to them all." We need grace to do this. With Jesus as our sponsor, He helps us to die to our selfishness. His security makes us secure. His truth confronts our lies and deceptions. How can we restore what we've stolen or lost? He will show us. How can we have interdependent rather than dependent relationships? Again, He will show us. Finally, we must be ready to act. After Jesus tells the story of the good Samaritan who demonstrates what love does, He tells the inquiring lawyer, "Go and do likewise" (Luke 10:37).

STEP NINE

"[We] made direct amends to such people wherever possible, except when to do so would injure them or others." Now that our moral inventory has identified the people we have harmed, it is time to act. We must be like Zacchaeus, the dishonest tax collector of Jericho, who, when called by Jesus, gave half of his goods to the poor and restored four times what he had stolen from others (see Luke 19:1-9). Likewise, alcoholics need to make amends by asking forgiveness for all the pain they have caused. They also need to repay bad loans and return stolen money. If they have alcoholic parents, they need to forgive them for their destructive influence.

Step nine builds barriers against the continuing ravages of our disease. It makes us accountable to people; we face how we have hurt each other. We experience the consequences of our behavior.

As we make amends, though, we must not act "when to do so would injure them or others." If we develop an emotional attachment to a woman who is not our wife, we need to confess this to God and to another person. We need to repent and renounce its perceived benefits. We also need to pray for God's forgiveness and healing, avoid intimate conversations and situations, and restore fidelity to our marriage. But to confess these feelings to the other woman and ask her forgiveness would probably injure her and others. It would likely create more intimacy. The confession of this sin to God, to our wife (depending on the security of our marriage) and to another person would be sufficient. Any other amends would probably be destructive and self-serving.

Making amends isn't easy. As Jesus sets us free, our actions testify to our freedom. Don't avoid this step for fear of hurting others. We are probably afraid of being hurt ourselves. Truth heals when spoken in love. Pray that the self-giving Jesus will free us to die to our false selves. His true self will shine through us. Pray for wisdom so that there won't be further damage. We never use restoration merely to relieve our guilt—making amends is primarily for other people's good. Only after we take this step for others are we able to grow and find freedom from future abuse.

A friend of mine lived the rock 'n' roll lifestyle in Hollywood. After picking up a girlfriend and moving in with her, he stole her credit card and ran up hundreds of dollars in bogus charges. Once he became a Christian, he shared this part of his past with me. We decided to go to her apartment and return the money. As we drove over together, we prayed in the car. When she came to the door, she was enraged to see him. Then she was staggered as he pulled out a roll of twenties and handed it to her. He asked her forgiveness for ripping her off and told her that Jesus had come into his life. As we drove away, she watched in shock. He left in joy. That was that. "Go and do likewise" (Luke 10:37).

STEP TEN

"[We] continued to take personal inventory and when we were wrong promptly admitted it." As we have said, the Christian life is crisis and process. Perfection is only in Jesus. It's not surprising that healing from addiction is mostly process. We need daily grace to detach ourselves from our idols and cross-addictions.

If we are honest, we are all vulnerable to relapse. As they say in A.A., relapse is a part of recovery. But as we look over our motives, relationships and behaviors and ask Jesus to heal us, we will move toward health. We must guard against becoming excessively introspective. As Martin Luther says, the Christian life is lived outside of ourselves—loving God and loving each other.[1] Self-giving comes through brokenness. When we are not self-giving, we are manipulative and self-serving. We need to keep our moral inventory current: *Lord, where am I in denial? Lord, what do You need to change in me? Lord, what are You doing in this painful situation?* and *How can I become more like You?* These prayers help us admit our wrongdoing.

We also need a community around us—people who know our sickness and who tell us when we are off course. Confession of sin, repentance for wrongdoing and renunciation of bogus benefits become habitual. We live by the forgiveness of our sins, given to us by our crucified and risen Lord. In this life, we always need His mercy poured out upon us.

STEP ELEVEN

"[We] sought through prayer and meditation to improve our conscious contact with God, as we understood Him, praying only for knowledge of His will for us and the power to carry that out." Again, Christianity is not a religion but a relationship with Jesus. Prayer inaugurates it, grows it and sustains it. Through prayer we welcome Jesus into our lives. Through prayer we walk with Him day by day. Through prayer we grow in intimacy with Him, becoming more like Him. Through prayer we welcome the Spirit's power in our lives. Indeed, prayer improves our "conscious contact" with God.

Meditation is another important means of improving our contact. We don't empty our minds like an eastern mystic. Rather, we fill them with the Word of God (see Ps. 1:2). A great place to start is by reading a psalm each day and using it as a basis for our own prayers. We also need to walk with Jesus through the Gospels and take the time to have Him teach us and see ourselves in the stories. As we wait on God to speak to us personally, being silent before Him, His Word tests the truth we hear.

Through prayer and meditation, we develop what John Wimber called a "secret history" with God. This grows, as Jesus says, when we go into the closet, shut the door and seek our heavenly Father (see Matt. 6:5-6). As we open more of ourselves to Him, He opens more of Himself to us. We enrich our lives with memories of our times with Him. We become more sensitive to His moment-by-moment leading. Our "Abba, Father" relationship with Him deepens, and with little self-consciousness, we become more like Him.

According to step eleven, we pray for two things: (1) the knowledge of God's will; and (2) the power to live it out. The institutional church tends to maximize the knowledge and minimize the power. No wonder so many of us continue in our addictions. But Christianity began with an explosion of power. The Holy Spirit empowered Jesus at His baptism. He promised the same power to His followers at Pentecost. In the book of Acts, as the Church grows, the power comes again and again. Paul wrote, "For the kingdom of God is not a matter of talk but of power" (1 Cor. 4:20). Down through the ages, in renewal and revival, the power of God falls. But rather than crying out to Him for another Pentecost, we live in our fears and in the illusion of our own control.

This is a time, however, when God is releasing the power of His Spirit upon the Church again. A fresh wind is blowing. The closed universe of our scientific worldview is under siege. How can we experience this power?

First, we need to believe that the Spirit's power is available for us today. Second, we need to repent of known sin, surrender control and pray for the power to come to us. If nothing happens immediately, we need to keep on praying. God may be testing our intentions. Are we serious? How will we use the power He gives us? Third, we need to visit places where the power of God is operating, lay aside our shame and ask for prayer. The Spirit's work is infectious—caught, not simply taught. We cannot manipulate God; His power is His to give.

Michael Cassidy, often called the Billy Graham of Africa, recounts his empowering experience that occurred during a renewal conference in South Africa. The biblical text about a grain of wheat dying in order to bear fruit hit him like a knife. He recounted:

Something deep and painful and crucifying and new was happening to me in those very moments. I could not restrain the tears. The grain of wheat which was my life had to die in new and deeper and truer ways if it was to bring forth fruit pleasing to God. . . . He wanted all of me. But the world, the flesh and the devil were still clutching. . . . It was painful to face. I had the Spirit, but did the Spirit have me?

I don't know how long the struggle continued. Half-an-hour. Maybe more. During that time loving brothers and sisters cared for me and prayed with me.

[That night] sleep would not come to me. Instead, quite out of the blue, the Spirit of praise came upon my soul. All seemed to be release. All seemed to be freedom. Hour after hour, I praised my God in unrestrained and

Christianity is no head trip. Only God's power saves us from religion, legalism and hypocrisy.

unrestrainable doxology and song. In words of men and angels I rejoiced. No fatigue visited me that night. All my senses were vibrantly alive to God. The Holy Spirit was blessing me. Wave upon wave, it seemed. Flow upon flow. He seemed to be bubbling up from within, surrounding from without, ascending from below, and descending from above!

Somewhere in the early hours of the morning I said to myself, "I don't know the correct biblical name for this, but this is the experience I've heard others talk of."[2]

Christianity is no head trip. Only God's power saves us from religion, legalism and hypocrisy. We have Jesus' word that if we who are evil know how to give good gifts to our children, how much more will our heavenly Father give the Holy Spirit to those who ask Him (see Luke 11:13; 24:49; Acts 1:8; 2:1-4; 10:44-46; 11:15-18).

If we can have intimacy with God, know how He wants us to live and receive His strength to do so, then we can go for it! This is the way to a selfless life with Jesus.

STEP TWELVE

"Having had a spiritual awakening as the result of these Steps, we tried to carry this message to alcoholics, and to practice these principles in all our affairs." Has God really changed our lives? Are we free to give ourselves away?

With Jesus as our sponsor, we have good news to share. We must pass on what God has done for us if we are to keep it. Otherwise, His gifts stagnate and we are then in danger of relapsing. Simply, this step calls for evangelism. Our recovery is not merely for ourselves; it is also for others' sake. As we share the Twelve Steps, our healing continues. Self-giving becomes our lifestyle.

We must also "practice these principles in all our affairs." They become part of the fabric of our lives. Consistency and maturity result. In everything, we admit our powerlessness, our inability to manage our lives and our insanity without Jesus as our higher power. Every area of our lives—our minds, wills and emotions; our relationships, activities and possessions; our identity and destiny—is His as we "turn our will and our lives over to the care of God." We continue our "searching moral inventory." We welcome confession, repentance, renunciation, accountability and making amends.

While we follow the Twelve Step guidelines, we remember that changes come by God's grace and His Spirit alone. He continues to remove our shortcomings. For this to happen, we must get closer to Him through prayer and meditation. We must ask for both the knowledge of His will and the strength to live it out. As we share these steps with others, we build them into our lives. Our addictions and codependences are broken. We become a part of the solution in this dysfunctional world. Our healing helps heal the Church. Our addictive culture's denial is broken as it is confronted with the truth that is lived out radiantly by the Body of Christ.

PUT IT ALL TOGETHER

As we follow the Twelve Steps with Jesus as our sponsor, we become more whole, more functional. *Fear goes* as we allow God to come into our lives and remove our sense of abandonment and our shame base. *Fear goes* as we detach from the addictive objects and desires that enslave us. *Fear goes* as we give up trying to control our lives, let down our false fronts and become honest about our moral failures. *Fear goes* as we expose what we have done to others and what they have done to us. *Fear goes* because the craving for security (the herd instinct) is now satisfied in Jesus and in companionship with His followers who are becoming more like Him.

Freedom comes as we receive God's forgiveness for our past, repent of our failures and set others free as we forgive them. *Freedom comes* as Jesus fills us with His love, freeing us to love others in nonaddictive and nonmanipulative ways. *Freedom comes* as we develop our conscious contact with God and pursue spiritual disciplines.

Self-giving results from our freedom from fear. We make amends to those we have wronged and share our lives with them. We offer others what we've found in our real relationship with Jesus—a way out of our addictions and codependences. Adventures and staggering challenges lie ahead in this new self-giving lifestyle. We are no longer lonely islands but communities of people in which our deepest needs are met and supported, and our broadest visions are fulfilled.

- Take the time to reflect on these last five steps.
- Which ones do you need to work on now?
- Which ones do you tend to pass over?
- Do any threaten you? Why?
- Where are you now in the whole sequence of the Twelve Steps?
- Are you applying them day by day?
- Pray that the Lord will bring to mind any people you have harmed.
- Ask Him to show you in what areas you have been justifying yourself.
- Is there anyone to whom you need to make amends? What plan do you have to do so?
- What plan do you have for keeping your moral inventory current? Who is holding you accountable for this?
- What is your plan for prayer and meditation? Do you have a plan for Bible reading? Do you have a place where you can go to seek the Lord? Make a plan and find a place if you don't.
- Are you submitted to God's will for your life? Are you listening for it in the Scriptures? Are you listening for the Holy Spirit to speak to you and lead you?
- Have you experienced the power of the Holy Spirit? Are

you seeking Him? Are you praying regularly for·Jesus to fill you with His Spirit?

- Whom have you shared the good news of your freedom in Christ with recently? Whom do you need to talk with? Make a plan.

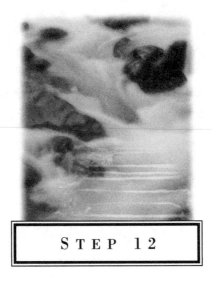

Connect

We're not meant to live life alone. We are created for relation-ships—loving God and loving each other. When Jesus calls us to Himself, He simultaneously calls us to each other. Paul wrote, "So in Christ we who are many form one body, and each member belongs to all the others" (Rom. 12:5).

When we isolate ourselves, we're sick. We must break through our selfishness, narcissism, perfectionism, fear of abuse, low self-esteem and all the other sins and wounds that keep us from each other. We must connect with people, with true community and with the world around us.

PEOPLE

We need people, but as it's often said, we can't get sober in a bar. If all of our primary relationships are with fellow addicts who are stuck in denial and feeding their cravings, we easily regress into our own sick behaviors. If our family and friends are dysfunctional, we continue to live in a toxic, shame-based atmosphere. We aren't to abandon them, leave home, get a divorce or reject those who love us. However, we need to find new relationships with people committed to physical, emotional and spiritual health. We need to connect with people who want to become more and more like Jesus. We need to be with others who make Him their sponsor. What might that mean?

Grace-Filled People

First, we need to connect with grace-filled people. A pastor friend of mine was considering hiring a new staff person. My first question to him was not "Is he talented, gifted or called?" but "Is he broken?" Out of our brokenness, we give up denial. Out of our brokenness, we welcome God's mercy and power into our lives. Out of our brokenness, God begins to rewire our damaged emotions. Out of our brokenness, we accept broken people. Out of our brokenness, we constantly receive and give grace. Out of our brokenness, we give up our hidden agendas, our "shadow selves" of hypocrisy and our seductive dealings. Out of our brokenness, we worship Jesus rather than money, sex, power, each other or even our own well-being. Look for and ask God for broken people and welcome them into your life.

True Worshipers

Second, we need to connect with true worshipers of Jesus. These are the people who have renounced their idols. These are the people who put Jesus first in their lives. These are the people whose eyes are on Him and who see the world and us through Him. Since we become like what we worship, these are the people who are becoming more like their Savior. These are the people who tell us the truth, who want us to be more like Jesus rather than more like them. These are the people who give us true security because their security is found in Him, not in our approval or support. Matt Redman described such worshipers:

> This world is full of fragile loves—love that abandons, love that fades, love that divorces, love that is self-seeking. But the unquenchable worshipper is different. From a heart so amazed by God and His wonders, burns a love that will not be extinguished. It survives any situation and lives through any circumstance. It will not allow itself to be quenched, for that would heap insult on the love it lives in response to.
>
> These worshippers gather beneath the shadow of the cross, where an undying devotion took the Son of God to His death. Alive now in the power of His resurrection, they respond to such an outpouring with an unquenchable offering of their own.[1]

Serious Disciples

Third, we need to connect with people who are committed to serious discipleship. We need people who make Jesus their sponsor. We need people who walk with Jesus day by day. We need people who love the Bible and live in its truth. We need people who know how to pray. We need people committed to community. We need people who care for the lonely, poor, afflicted and lost, and who love them unconditionally and bring them to Jesus. We need people who are delighted to give themselves away as they reflect the self-giving Jesus. They will be change agents in our lives. Henrietta Mears says, "If you want to learn how to pray, find someone who prays and pray with them. If you want to learn how to study the Bible, find someone who studies the Bible and study with them."[2] "Monkey see, monkey do." "Show and tell." It's that simple.

Lovers of Life

Fourth, we need to connect with people who love life. Jesus loves
life. He goes to parties. In a wedding crisis, He makes wine out of
water (see John 2:1-9). As we have seen in chapter 6, He refuses to
let His disciples fast. They are with the Bridegroom (see Mark
2:18-19). When He paints·the picture of the Father's love, the
prodigal son not only gets in the house, but there is also a celebration in his honor (see Luke 15:11-32). Jesus tells us that it is
party time in heaven when one sinner repents (see v. 24). His followers know that He is filled with joy. We need to be around
these kinds of people. The time for sour religion is over. The
time for grinding legalism is over. We need to learn to have good,
healthy fun again. We need to learn to laugh. We need to see that
true Christians enjoy life more than this addiction-saturated
culture. We need to be with people who take Jesus seriously
rather than themselves. Depending on our age and health, we
need to climb a mountain, enjoy a sunset, hear good music
(including rocking out), let art seep into our souls, read a good
book, cook a good meal, tell a good joke, play tennis, go surfing,
grab a skateboard, have friends over to watch a football game,
play computer games, go out to lunch, ride a horse, pet a dog,
hold a kitten, play with a child, watch Little League games, send
a text message—you get the picture. Some of us have to learn all
over again how to live life.

Spirit Led, Spirit Driven People

Fifth, we need to connect with people who are Spirit led and
Spirit driven. We need to connect with people who, in the
words of John Wimber, spell faith, "R-I-S-K." We need to connect with people who live on the edge of expectancy. We need
to connect with people who give away their sobriety to others.
We need to connect with people who are learning to pray for
the sick. We need to connect with people who welcome the

gifts of the Spirit and who see them operating in their lives. We need to connect with those who long for renewal and revival to come to the Church. We need to connect with those who serve the poor, reach the lost and hurt with those who hurt. We need to connect with people who are passionate for justice in an unjust world.

Honest People

Sixth, we need to connect with people who are honest about their own addictions. We need to be with people who want accountability for their struggles, temptations, relapses and idols. As A.A. says, "You are only as sick as your secrets." We need to be around people whom we trust and who trust us because we have surrendered our secrets. When shame goes, honesty comes, and we can be close to each other again.

Maturing People

Seventh, we need to connect with people who are changing, repenting and growing—people who don't have it all figured out. We need to connect with people who are Jesus focused rather than self-focused. We need to connect with people who allow the crisis to put them into process. We need to connect with people for whom Jesus is producing observed behavioral change. We need to connect with people who are recovering a rich emotional life. We need to connect with people who love themselves enough to hear the truth and love us enough to tell us the truth.

In summary, we need to connect with people whose deepest desire is to become more like Jesus. "Where the Spirit of the Lord is, there is freedom. And we, who with unveiled faces all reflect the Lord's glory, are being transformed into his likeness with ever-increasing glory, which comes from the Lord, who is the Spirit" (2 Cor. 3:17-18).

COMMUNITY

We need to connect with people who are committed to community. Lone rangers are bad role models. They don't know how to trust. They are afraid of exposure. They live in the illusion that they can do life on their own. They are preoccupied with their own control. They guard their own wounds. Yet when we come to Jesus, we give up control. For me this is at least an hourly issue as I pray *Lord, I give it up again to You.*

In the study of alcoholism, we learn that the family is the patient. In other words, the addict may begin the treatment, but all involved parties need to continue in it. Because our families are dysfunctional (at least to some extent), if we simply have them as our only context for healing, our wounding will continue. This is why Jesus gives us a new family, a new set of relationships, new connections with people.

As we connect with individuals, we also need to connect with a spiritual family. Be cautious around people who hate the Church, who criticize Christ's Body or who see the Church as exclusive rather than inclusive.

We are built for community: "It is not good for the man [or woman] to be alone" (Gen. 2:18). We all have the herd instinct. We learn who we are in relationships. The feedback and experiences of others help us to understand ourselves. Because of the brokenness of our past, we need new input from new people who are growing toward health—becoming more like Jesus.

In community, we break our isolation and gain a sense of belonging. In community, we are guarded against the assaults of the devil. In community, we are supported and nurtured. In community, we receive and give the gifts of the Spirit, designed to build us up. In community, we become accountable. In community, we have a network of relationships and role models, protecting us against codependency and against the distortions any single Christian might introduce into our lives. In community, Jesus' command that we love one another becomes practical. In community, we offer an alternative to the world's fractured and destructive relationships. In community, the presence of Jesus is manifested in our midst. In community, others can be introduced to Jesus in a very real and compelling way. In community, we are relieved from exclusive responsibility for each other and for new Christians. Through community, help is on its way. There is no alternative to living the Christian life.

We need people in our lives who want to grow toward health together. We need people who see that community life will allow them to become more like Jesus. Look for people who worship publicly and regularly, and who give their time, energy and money. They come not only to get but also to give. Their lives are becoming predictable and reliable and, paradoxically, more spontaneous and free. They also welcome newcomers. They have servants' hearts.

Our need for community is best fulfilled in small groups, with attendance of 10 to 12 people. The larger Body of believers must be broken down into these smaller fellowships, especially given our isolated and impersonal world. We need to meet weekly for authentic pastoral care and real Church discipline. Here we can risk exercising spiritual gifts such as prophecy ("I believe that God says to us tonight . . . "). We can risk being wrong and still be loved. We also can risk being right and not be prideful. Intimacy, ongoing relationships and real connections all come from small groups. As we join, we put ourselves under authority. We need to know that those who carry this ministry have broken servants' hearts. We need to know that they will not become spiritually abusive, seeking to control us or to use us for their success in ministry or for their own personal gain. We also need to experience functional leadership: no gossip, no half-truths, no manipulation, no forcing for the sake of spiritual experiences or spiritual power, no shaming, no guilt. We need leaders who confess their own addictions and idols, denouncing them regularly from the heart (without showcasing their humility or spirituality).

The dangers of connecting in community are twofold. For some, we idealize the community. For others, we become addicted to the community. We insist that it be the "New Testament Church" in its fullness. We want it to be what we missed in our family. We use it to meet our needs and get our way by putting the people around us under the law—the law of our "oughts" and "shoulds." "If you are real Christians, you should always be there for me. You ought to meet my every need. You ought to make me the center of the group and minister to me every week." In effect, "You should replace my dependency on Jesus and let me become dependent on you."

Our family of origin has its dysfunctional rules and roles. It is easy to carry them right into the Church and ruin our chances for real healing and growth. If we learned to manipulate out of anger, the fear of rejection or the fear of loss, we will do this instinctively in the Church. If we learned to abuse, seduce and overpower, we will act this out in our spiritual family. Whatever addiction or codependent behavior we bring to the Body of Christ, we need to want to be changed. This goes back to brokenness. It also goes back to our becoming more and more like Jesus, our sponsor. We need truth confrontations. We need hurts from the past to be healed. We need honest friends who love us unconditionally but who will not allow us to get away with our sin patterns any longer. Most of all, we need to let the Cross win in our marriages and in our relationships with our friends and with our brothers and sisters in Christ. As John Wimber often taught, "Forgiveness is the currency of the kingdom." This makes intimacy possible. We can risk hurting each other, speaking our minds, being wrong and even sinning against each other, because this drives us back to the Cross. Rather than bearing unresolved anger and a secret desire for revenge, we forgive from our hearts, learn from the pain and move on. Our goal is not codependent, addictive relationships. Our goal is mature, honest, interdependent relationships in which Jesus is the center of our worship, our hearts, our fearlessness, our freedom and our self-giving.

THE WORLD

We need to connect to the world for which Christ died. The best evangelists are often new Christians. Not only are they excited about their faith, but they also haven't lost their network of non-Christian friends. As new Christians or those in early recovery, we need to be wise about what we can handle. More mature Christians can help us in evaluating this. Again, we shouldn't try to get sober in a bar, but one primary purpose of our new community in Christ is to support us as we reach out to this lost world.

We are to be self-giving like the self-giving Jesus. When we make Him our sponsor, we learn to love as He loves. We ask Him to fill us with His Spirit: "God has poured out his love into our hearts by the Holy Spirit, whom he has given us" (Rom 5:5). Like Jesus, we learn to stop on the Jericho road and care for the wounded. One of love's skills is to learn to listen to people. This requires focus and concentration; let others do the talking. We must not interrupt them, using their thoughts to maneuver the conversation onto our own lives. We need not offer unsolicited advice. We must learn to ask questions and listen to the answers. However, the most loving thing we can do for people is to tell them that Jesus loves them. As we do this in a loving way, our manner will mirror our message.

Jesus calls us to subvert the world with its idols, corrupt values, lies, arrogance, lust and power trips. The simple way to do this is to tell the truth. Truth confronts the deception of Satan. Truth exposes the spin, the hype and the hidden agendas that keep us in bondage. Truth disarms the craving culture and the consumer messages playing in our craving brains. Truth exposes the manipulation of our lust, our inadequacies and our fears, which get us to try one more quick fix. Truth tells us that God made us in His image. Truth tells us that Jesus has come for us and that His kingdom is within reach. Truth tells us that Jesus heals, delivers and redeems. Truth tells us that He is now Lord. Truth will set us free. Tell the truth!

As we are honest about our struggles, people are free to be honest about theirs.

While we must tell the truth about Jesus, we also must tell the truth about ourselves. Truth tells us how valuable we are to Him. Truth tells us that we are loved unconditionally. Walking in the truth includes experiencing our heights and our depths, our joys and our sorrows, our craving and our healing. As we are honest about our struggles, people are free to be honest about theirs. We don't preach ourselves; we preach Christ and witness to His work in our lives. Evangelism is no power trip. It is, in the words of D. T. Niles, "One beggar telling another beggar where to find bread."[3] We need to be as honest about Jesus as we are about ourselves.

While we need to share Jesus' good news, we also need to demonstrate it. This means responding to people's felt needs. This means servant evangelism. This means taking the initiative

in our communities to care for children, the poor and the homeless. It means reaching out with the resources that God has
entrusted to us for a season. It means confronting racism or sex-
ism when it rears its ugly head. It means advocating justice for
those oppressed by poverty, crime, poor health care, gangs,
drugs and all the other ills that plague our nation. We need to
give away all that God has given to us. If we try to save our lives
or our churches, we will lose them. Jesus promises us this, and
He always tells the truth.[4]

Demonstrating the gospel includes more than acts of
mercy and justice. It means showing people their deepest
needs: to be free from the baggage of the past (guilt), the fear
of the future (death) and the ache of the present (loneliness,
the hole in the soul). It means showing people how Jesus meets
these needs. Our guilt has been canceled on the Cross. Our fear
of the future has been resolved by His resurrection. Our loneliness is shattered as He enters our lives and unites us to His
family.

IN CONCLUSION

Jesus is a receiver. He receives the Father's presence and purpose,
and so do we as we remain in intimate communion with Him.
Jesus is also a giver. He restores our fallen humanity, forgives our
sins, heals our diseases, drives out our demons and unites us to
Himself and to each other. By His example and by His Spirit, as
we make Him our sponsor, He teaches us how to live. In Him we
learn to be human again. We begin to live fearlessly, freely and
selflessly. This is what it means to be in communion with Jesus,
the one fully functional person.

As Jesus heals our inherited sin (generational) and cultural
sin (environmental), our personal sin becomes less and less
attractive to us. We become willing to let go of our addictive

attachments. As we become truly human again, we enter into bold worship, honest relationships, loving witness and Spirit-empowered works. Jesus' presence shines through our re-created humanity, and one day, we will be fully like Him. This was God's original design: "Let us make man[kind] in our image" (Gen. 1:26). This is our final destiny:

> Dear friends, now we are children of God, and what we will be has not yet been made known. But we know that when he [Jesus] appears, we shall be like him, for we shall see him as he is (1 John 3:2-3).

- Think about your connections: relationships, family and the larger world.
- Whom are you connected with now?
- Are they people who are moving toward health?
- Are they confronting their addictions honestly?
- Do they want to become like Jesus?
- What is your family like?
- Are you part of a Christian community?
- How does it function? What is your level of commitment?
- What role does forgiveness play in your fellowship?
- What are your connections with the outside world?
- Are they healthy?
- Are you conforming yourself to the world or are you changing it?
- How do you demonstrate the gospel?
- How equipped are you to talk to others about Jesus?
- Are you caring for the poor, the disadvantaged, the homeless and the marginalized?
- What form does that caring take? Ask Jesus to direct you in this area.

Endnotes

Step 1

1. Gerald May, *Addiction and Grace* (San Francisco: Harper and Row, 1988), p. 4.
2. Ibid.

Step 2

1. Gerald May, *Addiction and Grace* (San Francisco: Harper and Row, 1988), p. 4.
2. Drew Pinsky, *Cracked* (New York: HarperCollins, 2003), p. 54.
3. Ibid.
4. Ibid.
5. Ibid.
6. Ibid., p. 55.
7. Ronald Ruden, *The Craving Brain* (New York: HarperCollins, 1997), p. 48.
8. Ibid., p. 4.
9. Melody Beattie, *Codependent No More* (New York: Harper/Hazelden, 1987), p. 31.
10. Ibid.
11. Ibid.
12. Judith MacNutt, personal conversation with author, n.d.
13. Anne Wilson Schaef, *Co-dependence: Misunderstood-Mistreated* (San Francisco: Harper and Row, 1986), p. 4.
14. John Bradshaw, *Bradshaw on the Family* (Deerfield Beach, FL: Health Communications, 1988), p. 172.
15. May, *Addiction and Grace*, p. 3.
16. Ibid.
17. Ibid.
18. Ibid., p. 4.
19. Ibid., p. 3.
20. Tom Wright, *Bringing the Church to the World* (Minneapolis, MN: Bethany House, 1992), pp. 44-52.
21. Contrast Genesis 1:28 with Romans 1:24-27 and 1 Corinthians 6:9-11.
22. Ruden, *The Craving Brain*, p. 48.

Step 3

1. Drew Pinsky, *Cracked* (New York: HarperCollins, 2003), p. 55.
2. Ibid., p. 60.

3. Ronald Ruden, *The Craving Brain* (New York: HarperCollins, 1997), p. 27.

4. Pinsky, *Cracked*, p. 20

5. Ibid., p. 30.

6. Stanton Peele, *Love and Addiction* (New York: New American Library, 1975), p. 17.

7. Sharon Wegscheider-Cruse, "Co-Dependency: The Therapeutic Void," in *Co-Dependency: An Emerging Issue* (Pompano Beach, FL: Health Communications, 1984), p. 1, quoted in Anne Wilson Schaef, *Co-dependence: Misunderstood-Mistreated* (San Francisco: Harper and Row, 1986), p. 14.

8. Anne Wilson Schaef, *When Society Becomes an Addict* (San Francisco: Harper and Row, 1987), p. 15.

9. Anne Wilson Schaef, *Co-dependence: Misunderstood-Mistreated* (San Francisco: Harper and Row, 1986), p. 4.

10. John Bradshaw, *Bradshaw on the Family* (Deerfield Beach, FL: Health Communications, 1988), p. 6.

11. David Blankenhorn, *Fatherless America* (New York: Harper Perennial, 1996), p. 1.

12. Ibid.

13. Alice Miller, *For Your Own Good* (New York: Farrar Straus Giroux, 1984), p. ix.

14. Mic Hunter, *Abused Boys* (New York: Fawcett Books, 1990), p. ix.

15. Miller, *For Your Own Good*, p. 7.

16. Ibid.

17. Ibid, p. 87.

18. Ibid., p. xi.

19. Ibid., p. xvi.

20. Bradshaw, *Bradshaw on the Family*, p. 4.

Step 4

1. Dallas Willard, *The Divine Conspiracy* (San Francisco: HarperSanFrancisco, 1998), p. 41.

2. Bob Dylan and Tim Drummond, copyright 1980 Special Rider Music.

3. Drew Pinsky, *Cracked* (New York: HarperCollins, 2003), p. 19.

4. Ibid., p. 112.

5. Gershen Kaufman, *Shame, the Power of Caring* (Cambridge, MA: Schenkman Publishing Company, 1980), n.p., quoted in John Bradshaw, *Bradshaw on the Family* (Deerfield Beach, FL: Health Communications, 1988), p. 2.

6. John Bradshaw, *Bradshaw on the Family* (Deerfield Beach, FL: Health Communications, 1988), p. 2.

7. Ibid.

8. Gerald May, *Addiction and Grace* (San Francisco: Harper and Row, 1988), pp. 99-100.

Step 5

1. J. B. Phillips, *The New Testament in Modern English* (New York: Macmillan, 1959), p. 405.
2. Today he might go away to college.
3. Helmut Thielicke, *The Waiting Father* (New York: Macmillan, 1950), p. 22.
4. Helmut Thielicke, *The Waiting Father* (New York: Harper and Row, 1959), p. 28.

Step 6

1. Martin Luther, "The Freedom of a Christian," quoted in John Dillenberger, *Martin Luther: Selections from His Writings* (Garden City, NY: Anchor Books, 1961), p. 60.
2. Dietrich Bonhoeffer, *The Cost of Discipleship* (New York: Macmillan, 1963), p. 47.
3. Gerald May, *Addiction and Grace* (San Francisco: Harper and Row, 1988), p. 4.
4. C. S. Lewis, *Mere Christianity* (London: Collins, 1952), p. 172.
5. Rich Buhler, *Love: No Strings Attached* (Nashville, TN: Thomas Nelson, 1987), p. 25.
6. For more information, see Karl Barth, *A Shorter Commentary on Romans* (Richmond, VA: John Knox Press, 1959), pp. 24-54.

Step 7

1. Stanton Peele, *Love and Addiction* (New York: New American Library, 1975), p. 17.
2. Gerald May, *Addiction and Grace* (San Francisco: Harper and Row, 1988), p. 4.
3. Howell Harris, personal journal entry, June 18, 1735, quoted in Edward Morgan, *The Life and Times of Howell Harris* (London: Hughes and Butler, 1852), p. 10.
4. Drew Pinsky, *Cracked* (New York: HarperCollins, 2003), p. 62.

Step 8

1. C. S. Lewis, *Mere Christianity* (London: Fontana Books, 1952), p. 52.
2. Dietrich Bonhoeffer, *The Cost of Discipleship* (New York: Macmillan, 1963), pp. 135-138.
3. Ibid., pp. 139-141.
4. Dick Halverson (speech, Prison Fellowship banquet, San Diego, CA, November 15, 1990).

Step 9

1. Melody Beattie, *Codependent No More* (New York: Harper/Hazelden, 1987), p. 33.

2. Reinhold Niebuhr, *An Interpretation of Christian Ethics* (New York: Harper and Brothers, 1935), p. 17, quoted in Charles Kegley and Robert Bretall, eds., *Reinhold Niebuhr: His Religious, Social, and Political Thought* (New York: MacMillan, 1956), p. 53.

3. Francis MacNutt, sermon presented at Mt. Soledad Presbyterian Church, La Jolla, California, August 1983.

4. John Wesley, personal journal entry, January 1, 1739.

5. Dwight L. Moody, *Secret Power* (Ventura, CA: Regal Books, 1987), p. 17.

Step 10

1. Frank Buchman's definitive biography is by Garth Lean, *On the Tail of a Comet* (Colorado Springs, CO: Helmers and Howard, 1988).

2. *Alcoholics Anonymous*, 3rd ed. (New York: Alcoholics Anonymous World Services, 1976), pp. 59-60.

3. Gerald May, *Addiction and Grace* (San Francisco: Harper and Row, 1988), p. 96.

4. Ibid, p. 94.

5. Alice Miller, *For Your Own Good* (New York: Farrar, Straus and Giroux, 1984), p. 7.

6. John Bradshaw, *Homecoming* (New York: Bantam Books, 1990), p. xi.

Step 11

1. Martin Luther, "The Freedom of a Christian," quoted in *Martin Luther: Selections from His Writings*, ed. John Dillenberger, (Garden City, NY: Anchor Books, 1961), p. 80.

2. Michael Cassidy, *Bursting the Wineskins* (London: Hodder and Stoughton, 1983), pp. 117-122.

Step 12

1. Matt Redman, *The Unquenchable Worshipper* (East Sussex, UK: Kingsway Publications, 2001), p. 11.

2. Dr. Henrietta Mears, personal conversation with author, Forest Home camp, California, summer 1960.

3. D. T. Niles, lecture presented at Princeton Theological Seminary, Princeton, New Jersey, 1960.

4. On the Day of Judgment we will have to account for our care of the poor and persecuted, especially those in the Body of Christ, the least of the brothers and sisters (see Matt. 16:25; 25:31-46).

*For additional
information, visit:*

www.kingdomrain.net